TABLE OF CONTENTS

Top 20 Test Taking Tips

1. Carefully follow all the test registration procedures
2. Know the test directions, duration, topics, question types, how many questions
3. Setup a flexible study schedule at least 3-4 weeks before test day
4. Study during the time of day you are most alert, relaxed, and stress free
5. Maximize your learning style; visual learner use visual study aids, auditory learner use auditory study aids
6. Focus on your weakest knowledge base
7. Find a study partner to review with and help clarify questions
8. Practice, practice, practice
9. Get a good night's sleep; don't try to cram the night before the test
10. Eat a well balanced meal
11. Know the exact physical location of the testing site; drive the route to the site prior to test day
12. Bring a set of ear plugs; the testing center could be noisy
13. Wear comfortable, loose fitting, layered clothing to the testing center; prepare for it to be either cold or hot during the test
14. Bring at least 2 current forms of ID to the testing center
15. Arrive to the test early; be prepared to wait and be patient
16. Eliminate the obviously wrong answer choices, then guess the first remaining choice
17. Pace yourself; don't rush, but keep working and move on if you get stuck
18. Maintain a positive attitude even if the test is going poorly
19. Keep your first answer unless you are positive it is wrong
20. Check your work, don't make a careless mistake

US Postal Exam

Purpose

The General Entrance Test Battery 470 and 473 are used to fill all entry level career Processing, Distribution, and Delivery Post Office jobs. The process initially will be used for the five most populous entry-level positions — city carrier, mail handler, mail processing clerk, sales and services associate and sales, services and distribution associate - the vast majority of all fulltime jobs available with the Postal Service. The Battery 470 and the new 473 which will be discussed later are by far the most popular Post Office test exam given by the Postal Service. Thousands of people usually apply when it is offered.

Testing Frequency

The Battery 470 and the new Battery 473 are given by individual Postal districts on an as-needed basis. Some districts may give this Post Office the exam as often as twice a year, while others give it only once every few years. The exam results are used to fill both immediate and future openings until it is eventually given again.

All candidates who are interested in postal jobs as window/counter clerks, city carriers, distribution clerks, flat sorting machine operators, mail handlers, mail processors, mark-up clerks, and rural carriers are required to take the 470 exam before obtaining employment. Depending on the position, a candidate may also be required to take additional tests. The U.S. Postal Examination (470) is used by the Postal Service to evaluate job-related skills.

When a job opening has been announced, contact the CDC, the hiring post office, or your local post office for Form 2479. Once the post office has received your application, it will mail you information about the date, time, and place that the exam will be held.

How to Apply

When the Battery 470 or 473 is to be given in a particular area, the Postal Service first announces an application period that generally lasts only 5 - 10 days, but it can be as long as several months. Included in the announcement is a code number that identifies your specific testing event. To apply, you are instructed to call a toll free number where your information is taken via an interactive voice response system. During this phone call, you are required to enter the code number that identifies your specific testing event. You can only apply during the designated dates, and the code number is only valid during the designated dates. Postal policy requires that a notice be placed in the lobbies of all Postal facilities in the area to be tested. At the end of 2001, the Postal Service revised their application process so that you can apply online as well.

To apply for most basic postal positions you need to sign up to take the civil service exam, known as the 470 Battery Test, The test is for those who want to apply for the following positions: clerk, mail carrier, mail handler, mark-up clerk, mail processor, flat-sorting machine operator, and distribution clerk.

- Window Clerk: These are the people who serve you at the post office. This includes a variety of duties including selling stamps, weighing packages, preparing money orders, and answering your questions about USPS policies and services.
- Mail Carrier: City Carriers deliver mail to city businesses and residences. They usually have a certain route in which they deliver and pick up mail. Sometimes it is by foot and sometimes it is in a vehicle depending on their assigned area. Rural Carriers deliver and collect mail from rural businesses and residences. They have a wider variety of duties than City Carriers because they often have more direct contact with customers.
- Mail Handler: Mail Handlers load and unload mail from trucks and bins and help in sorting. They also cancel stamps.
- Mark-Up Clerk: Mark-Up Clerks work with mail that is undeliverable, correcting addresses, re-routing and/or returning mail.
- Mail Processor: Mail Processors run equipment that processes mail. They also help load and sort mail.
- Flat-Sorting Machine Operator: Sorting Machine Operators read zip codes to sort mail. They also load and unload mail.
- Distribution Clerk: Distribution Clerks begin the process of distributing mail. They sort mail by destination location.

If you are interested in applying for a post office job, you must first sign up to take the 470 or 473 Battery Test. Tests are given in areas of the state according to which post office districts are hiring.

The Application

It is usually a card, not much bigger than a postcard, that asks for basic information about you such as name, address, phone number, birth date, social security number, military status, etc. It is not long like most employment applications.

Scheduling Test Dates

Applicants are scheduled to take their Postal test exams several weeks after applying. They receive a scheduling notice by mail about two weeks before the Postal test date.

Difficulty of the Exam

The Battery 470 and its twin, the 473, are exceedingly difficult and rigidly timed Post Office exams. We are told that over 70% of all applicants fail their Post Office exams completely and that the average score for those who manage to pass is only a 76. The passing score is 70, and the highest possible score for non-veterans is 100. Applicants scoring below 70 are not considered for Post Office employment. Most experts agree that a score in the high 90's is needed to be called in for Post Office employment within a reasonable period of time.

Statement on Employment ©USPS

We are a large labor-intensive organization that recognizes our employees as one of our most important assets. Our successes and failures are largely determined by the caliber and efforts of our employees. In addition to our entrance examinations, the following eligibility requirements are used to determine employment.

Age Requirement

18 years at the time of appointment or 16 years with a high school diploma.

Citizenship

Employees must be a U. S. citizen or permanent resident alien.

Basic competency in English

Selective Service

Males born after 12/ 31/ 59 must be registered with the Selective Service System.

Employment History

Applicants must provide the names of their current employer and all previous employers for the 10-year period immediately preceding the date of application or to their 16th birthday, whichever is most recent.

Military Service

Military service is treated as prior employment. Veterans must indicate service and submit Copy 4 of the DD Form 214, Certificate of Release or Discharge from Active Duty.

Criminal Conviction History

A local criminal check is required prior to employment. A more extensive criminal history check is completed at employment.

Drug Screen

A qualification for postal employment is to be drug free, and is determined through a urinalysis drug screen.

Medical Assessment

A medical assessment is conducted to provide information about an applicant's ability to physically or mentally perform in a specific position.

Safe Driving Record

A safe driving record is required for employees who drive at work (i. e., city carriers, motor vehicle operators, etc.)

Postal Service exams, like test 473, are opened to the public to meet local staffing needs. Entry-level tests examine general aptitude and/or characteristics, not knowledge of facts. The test provides a screening process on job-related criteria for job applicants and allows applicants to compete for positions.

Test Day

- Make sure you are rested and have eaten a good meal.
- Go to the restroom before the test and try to limit your liquid intake. The test lasts 2-3 hours and you will not perform well if you are distracted or uncomfortable.
- Arrive early. If you are late you will not be admitted in the examination room. The rules are rigid on this matter. Whatever the scheduled time for your test is, that is the time the doors will be locked.
- Once you are there familiarize yourself with the surroundings and get comfortable.
- Choose the best seat for YOU. Choose a seat with good lighting that is away from distractions such as the door. In some cases seats are assigned upon arrival.
- Bring the scheduling package you received and a picture ID such as a driver's license. These will be checked at the door.
- Bring pencils.
- Work on each section of the test until you are instructed to stop. Every second counts. Be careful to begin and end as instructed or you will be disqualified.
- Mark the answer sheet clearly. A machine will score your answer sheet and stray marks or incomplete erasures may cause incorrect scoring.
- Remember to pace yourself for speed and accuracy.
- Be careful of distractions. Concentrate on what is in front of you.
- If you finish early, go back and check your answers in that section.

470 and 473 Battery Test
U.S. Postal Service

Battery 473

The Battery 473 exam begins its rollout to the field November, 2004. By July 2005, all offices will have offered the new exam. Existing registers can be used until the new exam is given for a facility — after that, all new hires must come from a Battery 473 register. Battery 473 combines measures of familiar favorites such as address checking, and coding and memory, with measures of other job-related behaviors such as identifying information needed to complete forms and demonstrating service orientation, conscientiousness and interpersonal skills.

Test 473 requires a minimum score of 70. Acceptable test scores range from 70 to 100 and are called the basic rating. Veterans' Preference Act of 1944 requirements may add points to the basic rating. If points are added, the basic rating is called the final rating.

A passing score on test 473 qualifies you to continue in the hiring process but does not guarantee employment with the Postal Service. If you qualify, Your name is listed on an entrance register - a resource to help the postal service consider applicants for vacant positions. Your name appears on the register with other applicants who passed the test.

By law, disabled veterans with passing scores are listed at the top of the register ahead of other applicants who passed the exam. All other veterans' preference applicants and nonpreference applicants are listed in descending order of their final ratings (with veterans' preference points added, if applicable). Veterans' preference applicants are listed ahead of nonpreference applicants with the same final rating.

The Postal Service must ensure the public's trust and confidence by maintaining the security and reliability of the mail. The public has the right to expect the Postal Service to maintain the privacy of the mail. Postal Service employees have the right to expect a safe environment in which to work. Thus, Postal Service employees must have integrity and be honest, trustworthy, reliable, and courteous.

Contents of entry-level battery 473

1 - Test Part	2- Number of Items	3- Time Allowed	4- Subject Matter Covered
Part A Address Checking	60	11 min.	Determine whether two addresses are the same.
Part B Forms Completion	30	15 min.	Identify information for correctly completing forms.
Part C Section 1 - Coding	36	6 min.	Identify the correct code to assign for an address.
Part C Section 2 - Memory	36	7 min.	Memorize codes to be assigned to a range of addresses.
Part D Personal Characteristics and Experience Inventory	236	90 min.	Tendencies toward job-related characteristics and experience.

Test Instructions

During the test session, it will be your responsibility to pay close attention to what the examiner has to say and to follow all instructions. One of the purposes of the test is to see how quickly and accurately you can work. Therefore, each part of the test will be carefully timed. You will not START until being told to do so. Also, when you are told to STOP, you must immediately STOP answering the questions. When you are told to work on a particular part of the examination, regardless of which part, you are to work on that part ONLY. If you finish a part before time is called, you may review your answers for that part, but you will not go on or back to any other part. Failure to follow ANY directions given to you by the examiner may be grounds for disqualification. Instructions read by the examiner are intended to ensure that each applicant has the same fair and objective opportunity to compete in the examination.

Address Checking

Address checking questions are probably the easiest questions on the exam. You will be given a list of correct addresses and a list of the same addresses, some of which will have minor errors. If the two addresses are alike, you will select "A" on your answer sheet; if they are different, you will select "D."

This section has 95 questions. Each question consists of 2 addresses. You will be given 6 minutes to compare these and mark your answer sheet. To get your score on this section subtract the number of wrong answers from the number of correct answers. The result is your score.*

Secret #1-Speed

Practice at a higher rate of speed than your normal comfort level. This will increase your pace by the time of the exam. Your ability and tolerance for speed will increase after repeated practice. Remember to keep the accuracy ratio high. You must be fast but accurate.

Secret #2-Preparation is an Advantage

Unlike others you will be prepared and know what is coming throughout the testing period. This should give you a level of comfort and confidence that will help you achieve a higher score.

Secret #3-Check answers if Time Allows

If you finish early check your answers. Make sure that the answer for #4 is marked on the answer sheet as #4. Check any addresses that you were unsure of.

Secret #4-Do Not Guess on this Section

Remember wrong answers will count against you in the scoring procedure. Your score will be reduced if you guess incorrectly.

Completing Tasks

Part B of test 473 consists of 30 items to be completed in 15 minutes. This is a test of your ability to identify information needed to complete forms similar to those used by the Postal Service. You will be shown several forms on this test, along with several items about what information is required to complete each form. Each part of the form is labeled (for example, 7 and 7a).

Scoring Answers

Your score for Part B of test 473 is based on the number of items that you answer correctly. There is no penalty for guessing on this part of the test. It is generally to your advantage to respond to each item, even if you have to guess.

Reducing Errors

Here are suggestions to help you reduce errors on Part B of test 473:

• Study each form carefully - Each of the forms in this test part is different and calls for different information in the various sections. You should take time to study the forms carefully before responding to the items to be sure that you know what information is desired.

• Consider answering items you know and answer other items later. If you return to an item, take extreme care to make sure that you are marking the correct answer on your answer sheet. It is easy to lose your place and darken the wrong circle.

• As time permits, go back and attempt to answer the more difficult items. If you have narrowed a difficult item down to one or two choices, you may want to make an educated guess.

Forms Completion Sample Questions

Look at the sample form and questions shown below. Please study the form and complete the sample questions. Mark your answers in the *Sample Answer Grid*.

Sample Form

1. Last Name		**2. First Name**
3. Street Address		
4. City	**5. State**	**6. ZIP Code**
7. Date 7a. Month 7b. Day 7c. Year		**8. Amount Paid** $

S1. Where should the last name be entered on this form?

A. Box 1

B. Box 2

C. Box 3

D. Box 4

S2. Which of these is a correct entry for Line 7a?

A. $62.30

B. 2005

C. August

D. 70455

Sample Answer Grid	
S1.	Ⓐ Ⓑ Ⓒ Ⓓ
S2.	Ⓐ Ⓑ Ⓒ Ⓓ

Completed Sample Answer Grid	
S1.	● Ⓑ Ⓒ Ⓓ
S2.	Ⓐ Ⓑ ● Ⓓ

*In the **Sample Form**, Box 1 is labeled "Last Name". Therefore, the correct answer for Sample Question 1 is "A. Box 1". In the **Sample Form**, Line 7a asks for a month, and April is the only month among the answer choices. Therefore, the correct answer for Sample Question 2 is "C. April". Notice that the **Completed Sample Answer Grid** on the right side of the page shows the correct responses filled in.*

Completing Exercise 2, Forms Completion

• Give yourself 7 minutes to complete this exercise. While this test part is designed to allow sufficient time to read and review each form, it is important to practice responding to the items within a reasonable time period.

• Read each form and answer the items based upon the information provided.

Exercise 2: Forms Completion

Sample Form 1

Attempted Delivery Notice	
1. Today's Date	**3a. Sender's Name**
2. Date Item(s) Sent	**3b. Sender's Address**
4. [] If checked, someone must be present at the time of delivery to sign for item(s)	
5. Enter number of each 5a. ____ Letter 5b. ____ Magazine/Catalog 5c. ____ Large envelope 5d. ____ Box	**6. Postage** 6a. [] If checked, there is postage due on the item(s) 6b. __________ Amount due
7. Delivery 7a. [] Item(s) will be redelivered tomorrow 7b. [] Please pick up the item(s) at your local Post OfficeTM. The item(s) will be available after: 7c. Date ________________ 7d. Time ________________	

1. Where would you enter the sender's address?

A. Box 1

B. Box 2

C. Box 3a

D. Box 3b

2. Which of these would be a correct entry for Box 2?

A. A check mark

B. "11-12-04"

C. "4"

D. "Renae Smith"

3. You could enter a date in each of the following boxes EXCEPT which?

A. Box 1

B. Box 2

C. Line 5a

D. Line 7c

4.Which of these would be a correct entry for Line 7d?

A. "PO Box 454 Robert, LA 70455"

B. A check mark

C. "03/15/05."

D. "$10:00 a.m."

5. Where would you indicate that the customer must pick up the item at the Post Office?

A. Box 43a

B. Box 5a

C. Box 6b

D. Box 7b

6. Which of these would be a correct entry for Box 3a?

A. "Lydia Traylor"

B. "A check mark"

C. "5453 Essen Lane Baton Rouge, LA 70809"

D. "$5.08"

7. How would you indicate that there are two boxes to be delivered?

A. Enter "2" in Line 5a

B. Enter "2" in Line 5b

C. Enter "2" in Line 5c

D. Enter "2" in Line 5d

Sample Form 2

Mass Mailing Receipt	
1. Date	**4. Name of Permit Holder**
2. Post OfficeTM ZIP CodeTM	**5. Address of Permit Holder**
3. 5-digit Permit Number	**6. Telephone Number of Permit Holder**
7. Processing Category (check one) 7a. [] Letters 7b. [] Flats 7c. [] Automation Flats 7d. [] Parcels	**8. Total Number of Pieces**
	9. Total Weight
	9a. ___ pounds 9b. ___ ounces
	10. 2-digit Cost Code
	11. Total Paid $ ___________

8. Luke Strait holds the mass mailing permit. Where would you indicate this?

A. Box 3

B. Box 4

C. Box 5

D. Box 6

9. Where would you indicate that 75,000 pieces were sent?

A. Box 3

B. Box 8

C. Line 7a

D. Line 10

10. How would you indicate that the processing category is "Automation Flats"?

A. Put a check mark in Box 7a

B. Put a check mark in Box 7b

C. Put a check mark in Box 7c

D. Put a check mark in Box 7d

11. The total paid was $407.59. Where would you indicate this?

A. Box 6

B. Line 9a

C. Box 10

D. Line 11

12. Which of these would be a correct entry for Box 5?

A. "111 Lake Front Drive Miramar Beach FL 32550"

B. "Berry Town Candies"

C. "2/10/04"

D. A check mark

13. Which of these would be a correct entry for Box 10?

A. "30454"

B. "901-866-5243"

C. "30"

D. "70005-6320"

14. The Post Office ZIP Code is 77706. Where would you indicate this?

A. Box 1

B. Box 2

C. Box 3

D. Box 9

15. A number would be a correct entry for every box EXCEPT which?

A. Box 3

B. Box 4

C. Box 8

D. Line 11

Forms Completion Answer Key

1. D
2. B
3. C
4. D
5. D
6. A
7. D
8. B
9. B
10. C
11. D
12. A
13. C
14. B
15. B

Completing Tasks

Part C of test 473 consists of two sections. The Coding section consists of 36 items to be completed in 6 minutes. The Memory section consists of 36 items to be completed in 7 minutes.

This is a test of your ability to use codes quickly and accurately, both with a coding guide visible and from memory without using a guide. You will be shown a coding guide, along with several items that must be assigned a code. You must look up the correct code for each item and write your response on the answer sheet accurately and quickly. During the first section of the test part, you will be allowed to look at the coding guide while you assign codes. During the second section of the test part, you must assign codes based on your memory of the same coding guide. While the coding guide is visible, try to memorize as many of the codes as you can. These are the same codes that will be used in the memory section.

Note: During the actual test:

- You are not allowed to look at the codes when answering the items in the Memory section.

- You are not allowed to write down any addresses during the memorization period.

Memory

Memory for addresses questions are often considered one of the hardest parts of the exam. You will be given a set of boxes, each of which will contain addresses and names. After memorizing the content in the boxes, you will have to recall in which box each appeared.

Secret #1–Memorize Horizontally

Memorize the addresses horizontally, not vertically. This is more natural and will flow more easily for you.

Secret #2-Answer the Questions in This Section in Order

Answer all in order. Do not attempt to go through this section twice. There is not enough time for you to answer the ones that you think are easy and then attempt to go back and answer the others.

Secret #3-Speed

Practice at a higher rate of speed than your normal comfort level. This will increase your pace by the time of the exam. Your ability and tolerance for speed will increase after repeated practice. Remember to keep the accuracy ratio high. You must be fast but accurate.

Scoring Answers

Your score for Part C of test 473 is based on the number of items that you answer correctly minus 1/3 of the number of items you answer incorrectly. In both sections of this test part, your score depends on how many items you can correctly assign a code in the time allowed. You may not be able to assign a code to all of the items before time runs out, but you should do your best to assign codes to as many items as you can with a high degree of accuracy. There is a penalty for guessing on this test. It won't be to your advantage to guess randomly. However, if you can see that one or more responses is clearly incorrect, it will generally be to your advantage to guess from among the remaining responses.

Reducing Errors

On the test, you have several opportunities to work with the coding guide and practice memorizing the codes for each range of addresses before answering items on them based upon memory. Listen to the administrator's instructions. Do not become frustrated or discouraged - remain focused. Here are more suggestions to help you reduce errors on Part C of test 473:

- **Answer items you know** and answer other items later. Remember that you have a time limit for completing the items.

- **As time permits, go back and attempt to answer the more difficult items.** If you have narrowed a difficult item down to one or two choices, make an educated guess. If you return to an item, take care to make sure that you are marking the correct answer on your answer sheet. It is easy to lose your place and mark the wrong circle.

- **Arbitrarily guessing will probably not help your score.** If you can eliminate one or more of the answers, it may be to your advantage to guess.

- **Work as quickly and accurately as possible.** You are not expected to answer all items in the time allowed.

- **Fully use the practice opportunities and memorization periods you are given to practice memorizing the codes.**

Completing Exercise - Coding

- Move through items 1 through 15 and assign codes to each based upon the Coding Guide. Work as quickly and as accurately as possible.

- Time yourself on this exercise. You should stop after 2 minutes. You may not be able to finish all of the items in this exercise in that time, but practicing with a time limit will give you a better feel for taking the actual test.

When you finish exercise set 3, check your answers.

Exercise: Coding

CODING GUIDE	
Address Range	**Delivery Route**
1 - 99 Richoux Rd. 10 - 200 Hoffman Ave. 5 - 15 E 6th Street	A
100 - 200 Richoux Rd. 16 - 30 E 6th Street	B
10000 - 12000 Byers Lane. 1 - 10 Rural Route 1 201 - 1500 Hoffman Ave.	C
All mail that doesn't fall in one of the address ranges listed above	D

	Address	Delivery Route
1.	7 Richoux Rd.	A B C D
2.	102 Norwood Ave.	A B C D
3.	23 E 6th Street	A B C D
4.	16 E 6th Street	A B C D
5.	29 Richoux Rd.	A B C D
6.	8 Rural Route 1	A B C D
7.	1308 Hoffman Ave.	A B C D
8.	5 Rural Route 11	A B C D
9.	10191 Byers Lane	A B C D
10.	8 E 6th Street	A B C D
11.	183 Ridgeline Rd.	A B C D
12.	12050 Byers Lane	A B C D
13.	8 E 6th Street	A B C D
14.	1043 Hoffman Ave.	A B C D
15.	105 Richoux Rd.	A B C D

Coding – Answer Key

1. A
2. D
3. B
4. B
5. A
6. C
7. C
8. D
9. C
10. A
11. D
12. D
13. A
14. C
15. B

Completing Exercise - Memory

In this section of the test, you will assign codes based on your memory of the Coding Guide. You will use the same Coding Guide you have been using throughout this exercise.

• Take 3 minutes to memorize the Coding Guide.

• You should not take any notes when memorizing the Coding Guide, but you may write in the test booklet while you are answering the items.

Complete Exercise - Memory.

• Move through the items and assign codes to each based upon your memory of the Coding Guide. Do NOT refer to the Coding Guide as you work through this exercise. Work as quickly and as accurately as possible.

• You should not be able to see the Coding Guide during the exercise, and you should not turn back to an earlier page to look at it.

• Time yourself on this exercise. You should stop after 3 minutes. You may not be able to finish all of the items in this exercise in that time, but practicing with a time limit will give you a better feel for taking the actual test.

When you finish the exercise, check your answers against the correct ones.

Exercise - Memory

	Address	Delivery Route
16.	12 E. 6th Street	A B C D
17.	1494 Hoffman Ave.	A B C D
18.	255 Richoux Rd.	A B C D
19.	165 Richoux Rd.	A B C D
20.	7 Rural Route 1	A B C D
21.	17 Rural Route 1	A B C D
22.	28 E 6th Street	A B C D
23.	14 E 6th Street	A B C D
24.	4500 Byers Lane	A B C D
25.	5 N 6th Street	A B C D
26.	39 Richoux Rd.	A B C D
27.	151 Richoux Rd.	A B C D
28.	8 E 6th Street	A B C D
29.	205 Hoffman Ave.	A B C D
30.	11001 Byers Lane	A B C D

Memory – Answer Key

16. A
17. C
18. D
19. B
20. C
21. D
22. B
23. A
24. D
25. D
26. A
27. B
28. A
29. C
30. C

Part D: Personal Characteristics and Experience Inventory

Completing Tasks

Part D of the test consists of 236 test items to be completed in 90 minutes. The items in this test part check several personal characteristics, tendencies, or experiences related to performing effectively as an employee of the Postal Service.

Read each item carefully, and decide which of the response choices is most true about **you**. For some items, more than one response may describe you. However, be sure to mark one and only one response for each item. It is important to respond to each item, even if you are not completely sure which response is best. Also, it is generally best to work at a fairly fast pace.

Whenever possible, respond to the items in terms of what you have done, felt, or believed in a work setting. If you cannot relate the item to your work experiences, base your response on other experiences that are similar to work, such as school or volunteer activities. For example, if an item involves how often you have gotten into arguments with others, respond in terms of how often you have gotten into arguments with co-workers. If you have not held a job before, or if the item cannot be related to your work experiences, draw on whatever experiences are necessary to choose the response choice that best describes you.

This part of the test is divided into three sections. One section includes items with four response choices, ranging from "Strongly agree" to "Strongly disagree". Another section includes items with four response choices ranging from "Very often" to "Rarely or never". The final section includes items with anywhere from four to nine response choices.

Scoring Answers

Your score for Part D of test 473 is based on your responses to the items in this section. This test part calls for your honest responses. Dishonest self-descriptions are not to your advantage. All responses you give will be considered in determining your results.

Reducing Errors

Here are suggestions to help you reduce errors on Part D of test 473:

- **Read each statement carefully before marking your responses.**

• **There is no particular advantage to practicing your responses to these statements.** You should read each statement carefully and respond based upon your personal experiences or preferences.

Sample Question from Agree/Disagree Section

You like having your work interrupted.

A. Strongly Agree

B. Agree

C. Disagree

D. Strongly Disagree

Sample Question from Frequency Section

You do not plan things in advance.

A. Very often

B. Often

C. Sometimes

D. Rarely

Sample Question from Experience Section

The items in this section of the test assess your experience in areas related to performing effectively as an employee of the Postal Service.

Read each item carefully, and decide which of the response choices best describes your experience. Although for some items, more than one statement may describe your experience, be sure to mark only one response for each item.

What type of work do you like the least?

A. tasks that require sitting or standing in one place for hours

B. tasks that require working at a very fast pace

C. tasks requiring too many decisions

D. doing the same thing day after day

E. would not mind doing any of these

F. not sure

There is no exercise for Part D.

Practice Test

Part A-Address Checking

In this part of the test you will have to decide whether the two addresses are alike or different. You will have 11 minutes to answer 60 questions. Write A for alike or D for different on a separate sheet of paper. Remember to use the Test Secrets for the Address Checking Section.

• Move through the rows by checking the **List to be Checked** against the **Correct List**. Work as quickly and as accurately as possible.

Note: You may find errors in numbers, abbreviations, and words - all types of address-checking errors.

Your task is to:

• Compare numbers, abbreviations, and words in addresses and ZIP codes.

• Determine if each block (either address or ZIP code) is correct or incorrect.

• Mark A, B, C, or D, respectively for **No Errors**, errors in the **Address Only**, errors in the **Zip Code Only**, or errors in **Both** the address and ZIP code.

Exercise Set 1: Address Checking

A. No Errors

B. Address Only

C. ZIP Code Only (including city and state name)

D. Both

The questions are set up as: Address Line

Zip Code Line (including City, State)

Part A-Address Checking – 1

	Correct List	List to be Checked
1.	7172 S. 48th St Yakima WA 10345	7172 S. 48th St Yakima WA 10345
2.	3818 Morningview Cape Mobile, AL 36609-3652	3018 Morningview Cape Mobile, AL 36609-3852
3.	6579 22nd St. Wilson, Delaware 19886	6795 S 22nd St Wilson, Delaware 19886
4.	3817 Northingham Rd Atlanta, GA 30348-5503	3817 Northingham Rd Atlanta, GA 30348-5503
5.	8777 Courthouse Pl Bethesda MD 20816	8777 Courthouse Pl Bethesda MD 20816
6.	4608 E. Firetower Rd. Melbourne Fl 21907	4608 E. Firepower Rd. Melbourne Fl 21907
7.	5378 Bayou Oaks Ct Stamford, CT 06905-0125	5378 Bayou Oates Ct Stamford, CT 06905-0126
8.	4161 Patricia Ln Waterloo, Iowa 50703	4161 E. Patricia Ln Waterloo, Iowa 50703
9.	1579 W. Guardian Way TERRYTOWN ,LA 70056	1579 W. Guardian Way TERRYTOWN ,LA 70056
10.	9060 Oceanspray Jct Poolesville MD 20837-0250	9060 Oceanspray Jct Poolesville MD 20807-0250
11.	1620 Hesper Ave Montpelier VT 98326	1620 Hesper Ave Montpelier VT 98326
12.	1021 Gorenflo Pt Grand Island NE 59487	1012 Gorenflo Pt Grand Island NE 59487
13.	4969 Heatherwood Ln Little Rock AL 81415	4969 Heatherwood Ln Little Rock AK 81415

14.	6547 W Hanover St Louisville KY 38920	6547 E Hanover St Louisville KY 38029
15.	9567 Foxworthy Ct Fredrick MD 42995-0011	9567 Foxworthy Ct Fredrick MD 42995-0011
16.	1474 Tally Ho Cir Bettendorf IA 29571	1474 Tally Howard Cir Betteroff IA29571
17.	6357 W 69th Ave Augusta ME 41939	6357 W 69th Ave Augusta ME 41393
18.	9811 N Musella Ave Laredo TX 48930	9811 N Moosella Ave Lansing MI 64601
19.	7737 Cambridge Pl Detroit MA 48207	7737 Cambridge Pl Detroit MI 48207
20.	7980 Swallow Ave El Paso TX 92835-7802	7980 Swallow Ave El Pasco TX 92835-7802
21.	1903 W El Bonito St Superior WI 50667	1903 W El Burito St Superior WI 50667
22.	5599 Porter Pl Los Angeles CA 14157	5599 Porter Pl Las Angles CA 14157
23.	408 E Magnolia Dr Sacramento CA 94654	409 E Magnolia Dr Sacramento CA 94654
24.	5038 Heatherstone Pt Dallas Tx 96281-0152	5038 Heatherstone Pt Dallas TX 96261-0152
25.	7519 Arbor Vista Dr NEW ORLEANS LA 70122	7519 Arbor Vista Dr NEW ORLEANS LA 70122
26.	1516 Thorton Ave Wilkes-Barre PA 84217	1516 Thorton Bay Wilkes-Barre PA 84712
27.	6473 Byers Rd. Oklahoma City, OK 73149	6473 Byers Rd. Oklahoma City, OK 73149
28.	6876 E 54th St Flagstaff AZ 64821	6876 E 54th St Flagstaff AZ 64821
29.	2655 Englewood Rd	2655 Englewood Rd

	Saginaw, MI 48601	Staginaw, MI 48601
30.	3709 W Pineview Pl Roselle, N J 07203	3709 E Pineview Pl Roselle, N J 07203
31.	9860 Plantation Rd. Butte MT 54965-9860	9860 Planter Rd Butte MT 59965-9860
32.	4050 Llwellyn Grv Horn Lake, MS 38637	4050 Llwellyn Garden Horn Trail, MS 38637
33.	8950 N Badwin Ave Youngstown, OH 44507	8950 N Baldwin Ave Youngstown, OH 44507
34.	5673 Bonner Blvd Burke, VA 22015-9022	5673 Bonner Blvd Burke, VA 22015-9052
35.	4441 W Hollings Rd Kenosha WI 10590	4444 W Hollings Rd Kenosha WY 10590
36.	4135 E O'Neal Rd Kingman, AZ 86402-0120	4135 E O'Neal Rd Kingman, AZ 86402-0120
37.	3100 Abbey Ct Havertown PA 19083	3001 Abbey Ct Favertown PA 19083
38.	3054 Callaghan Cove Paradise TX 76073	3054 Callaghan Cove Paradise TX 76073
39.	3945 Richoux Rd. Las Cruces NM 64603	3954 Richoux Rd. Las Cruces NM 64603
40.	8950 Freeman Bld Mishawaka, IN 46544-1441	8950 Freeman Bld Mishawaka, IN 46544-1414
41.	4957 Humperdinck Pl Miami, FL 33135-0130	4957 Humperdickle Pl Miami, FL 33135-0130
42.	3340 Marco Polo Pt Edison, NJ 08820-0820	3340 Marco Polo Pt Edison, NJ 08820-0820
43.	9747 McCracken Ln Fort Wayne, IN 46835-0153	9747 McCracken Ln Port Wayne, IL 46835-0153
44.	1184 Mohammed Bay	1184 Mohammed Bay

	JACKSONVILLE,FL 32216	JACKSONVILLE,FL 32216
45.	6172 Powhaten Denver, Co. 80207-0256	6172 Powhatten Denver, Co. 80207-0256
46.	8211 N 52nd Ave Jacksonville, Fl 32241-4886	8211 S 52nd Ave Jacksonville, Fl 32241-4886
47.	9172 Morrison Way Glen Burtie MD 21061-6233	9172 Morrison Way Glen Burnie MD 21061-6233
48.	2828 Parkman Ave Jacksonville Bch FL 32250-5310	2828 Parkman Ave Jacksonville Bch FL 32250-5310
49.	4527 Aleutian Isle Doylestown PA 18901	4527 Aleutian Isle Doylestown PA 18901
50.	6800 S Welford Blvd Louisville, KY 40272	6800 N Welford Blvd Louisville, KY 40272
51.	5807 Berkeley Pt Bonifay, FL 32425	5807 Berkeley Pt Bonifay, FL 32425
52.	831 Belgrade Cove Webb City, MO 64870-8189	831 Belgrade Cove Webb City, MO 64870-8189
53.	4504 E Ponchatoula Blvd Baton Rouge LA 70818-6603	4504 E Ponchatoula Blvd Baton Rouge LA 70888-6603
54.	5000 Bermuda Bay Herndon, VA 20171-1925	5000 Bermuda Beach Herndon, VA 20171-1925
55.	1825 W Tulane Ave MARRERO, LA 70072-0072	1825 W Tulane Ave MARRERO, LA 70072-0072
56.	2309 Pinehaven Cove Onaga, KS 66521-6521	2309 Pinehaven Cove Omaha, KS 66521-6521
57.	9417 Meadowlark Pl Miami, FL 33155-6629	9417 Meadowlark Pl Miami, FL 33155-6629
58.	7172 Rebecca Cove San Diego, CA 92173-1550	7712 Rebecca Cove San Diego, CA 92173-1550
59.	5699 N 93rd Blvd Eaton, CO. 80615	5699 N 93rd Bay Eaton, CO. 80615

60.	3303 Demonica Rd. El Toro, CA 92609	3303 Demonica Rd. El Toro, CA 92609

Answers – Address Checking - 1

1. A
2. D
3. B
4. A
5. A
6. B
7. D
8. B
9. A
10. C
11. A
12. A
13. C
14. D
15. A
16. D
17. C
18. D
19. A
20. C
21. B
22. C
23. B
24. A
25. A
26. D
27. A
28. A
29. C
30. B
31. D
32. D
33. B
34. C
35. D
36. A
37. D
38. A
39. B
40. C
41. A
42. A
43. C
44. A
45. B
46. B
47. C
48. A
49. A
50. B
51. A
52. A
53. C
54. B
55. A
56. C
57. A
58. B
59. B
60. A

Address Checking Test – 2

1.	7172 W 48th St Hammond LA 70455	7172 S. 48th St Hammond LA 70455
2.	3818 Morningview Cape Little Rock AR 81415	3018 Morningview Cape Little Rock AK 81415
3.	6579 22nd St. Marquez, TX 77865-9988	6795 S 22nd St Marquez, TX 77865-9898
4.	3817 Northingham Rd Norton, Ma. 02766-0122	3812 Northingham Rd Norton, Ma. 02766-0122
5.	8777 Courthouse Bay San Luis Obispo, CA 93401	8777 Courthouse Pl San Luis Obispo, CA 93401
6.	4608 E. Firetower Rd. Lewisville, TX 75067	4608 E. Firetower Rd. Lewisville, TX 75067
7.	212 W Beach Blvd Melbourne Fl 21907	212 W Beach Blvd Melbourne Fl 22907
8.	5378 Bayou Oaks Ct Spring Hill , FL 34609-4609	5378 Bayou Oates Ct Spring Hill , FL 34609-4669
9.	4161 E. Patricia Ln Cerro Gordo, NC 28430-0182	4161 E. Patricia Ln Cerro Gordo, NC 28430-0182
10.	1579 W. Guardian Way Wing Gap, PA 18091	1579 W. Guardian Way Wind Gap, PA 18091
11.	9060 Traylor Jct Montpelier VT 98326	9060 Traylor Jct Montpelier VT 98325
12.	1620 Hesper Ave Mableton, GA 30126-0206	1620 Vesper Ave Mableton, GA 30126-0256
13.	1021 Worenflower Pt Warren Center, PA 18851-1881	1012 Worfenflower Pt Warren Center, PA 18851-1881
14.	4969 Heatherwood Ln St. Paul, MN 55107-5589	4969 Heatherwood Ln St. Paul, MN 55107-5589

15.	6547 W Hanover St Louisville KY 38920	6547 E Hanover St Louisville KY 38029
16.	9566 Foxworthy Ct South Holland IL 60473	9567 Foxworthy Ct South Holland IL 60473
17.	1474 Tally Ho Cir Torrington, CT 06790-0020	1474 Tally Howard Cir Torrington, CT 06790-0020
18.	1975 Northridge Dr. Fredrick MD 42995	1975 Northbridge Dr Fredrick MD 42995
19.	6088 W Primas Pl Lancaster, PA 17604-9091	6880 W Primus Pl Lancaster, PA 17604-9091
20.	1040 Navaho Tr Hartland, VT 05052-0048	1040 Navaho Pl Hartland, VT 00052-0048
21.	6357 W Second Ave NY, NY 10005-3198	6357 W Second Ave NY, NY 10005-3198
22.	9811 N Musella Ave Laredo TX 48930	9811 N Moosella Ave Lansing MI 64601
23.	7717 Cambridge Pl Kirtland Ohio 44094	7727 Cambridge Pl Kirtland Ohio 44094
24.	23145 Oak Street Cantonment, FL 32533	23145 Oak Street Cantonment, FL 32533
25.	1903 W El Bonito St Mobile, AL 36604-0040	1903 W El Burito St Mobile, AL 36604-0040
26.	5599 Porter Place Los Angeles CA 14157	5599 Porter Park Las Angles CA 14157
27.	1202 W Marketsville Lewistown, PA 17044	1202 W Marketsville Lewistown, PA 17074
28.	1103 N Belair St Geyworth, IL 61745	1103 W Belair St Geyworth, IL 61745
29.	1911 Sheffield Place Bettendorf IA 29571	1911 Sheffield Place Betteroff IA 29571

30.	408 E Magnolia Dr Holt, FL 32564	409 E Magnolia Dr Colt, FL 32564
31.	5038 Heatherstone Pt Virginia Beach, VA 23452	5038 Heatherstone Pt Virginia Beach, VA 23452
32.	20074 Commissary Rd Brooklyn, New York 11233-4502	2004 Commissary Rd Brooklyn, New York 11233-4502
33.	7519 Arbor Vista Dr Minturn, AR 72445-4454	7519 W Arbor Vista Dr Minturn, AR 72445-4455
34.	3176 W Travel Tr Grand Island NE 59487	3176 E Travel Tr Grand Island NE 59487
35.	8766 Columbia Cir Augusta ME 41939	8766 Columbia Cir Augusta ME 41393
36.	1516 Orange Ave Shobonier, Il 62885	1516 Orange Bay Shobolier, Il 62885
37.	6473 Byers Rd. Cape Coral, Florida 33990	6473 Byers Rd. Cape Coral, Florida 33990
38.	3313 E 54th St Flagstaff AZ 64821	3313 E 54th St Flagstaff AZ 64821
39.	2655 Englewood Dr Trumbull, CT 06611-6611	2655 Englewood Dr Trumbull, CT 06611-6161
40.	3709 W Pineview Pl Deming, NM 88030-3552	3709 E Pineview Pl Deming, NM 88030-3552
41.	9860 Plantation Rd. Bay Shore, NY 11706-7357	9860 Planter Rd Bay Shore, NJ 11706-7357
42.	2009 Lovers Lane Butte MT 54360	2009 Lovers Lane Butte MT 54366
43.	4547 Popps Ferry Rd. Ardmore, Pa 19003 -0922	4547 Bopps Ferry Rd. Ardmore, Pa 19003-0922

44.	3303 Demonica Rd. Danvers, MA 01923-0020	3303 Delmonica Rd. Danbury, MA 01923-0020
45.	8950 N Baldwin Ave El Frida, AZ 85610-8956	8950 N Baldwin Ave El Frida, AZ 85610-8958
46.	1131 Twin Cedar Ave Detroit MI 48207	1131 Triple Cedar Ave Detroit MI 48201
47.	9747 McCracken St Dallas Tx 96261	9747 McCracken St Dallas TX 96261
48.	4441 W Hollings Rd Kenosha WI 10590	4444 W Hollings Rd Kenosha WY 10590
49.	9172 Morrison Ct Sacramento CA 94654-1454	9172 Morrison Cv Sacramento CA 94654-1454
50.	5800 Berkeley Pt Wilkes-Barre PA 84217-0112	5800 Berkeley Pt Wilkes-Barre PA 84712-0112
51.	2309 Pinehaven Cove El Paso TX 92835	2309 Pinehaven Cave El Paso TX 92835
52.	3945 Richoux Rd. Las Cruces NM 64603	3954 Richoux Rd. Las Cruces NM 64603
53.	6357 W Marina Ave Superior WI 50667	6357 W Martina Ave Superior WI 50667
54.	4135 E O'Neal Rd Moultrie, Georgia 31788	4135 E O'Neal Rd Moultrie, Georgia 31738
55.	3100 Abbey Ct Maple heights, Ohio 44137-2007	3001 Abby Ct Maple heights, Ohio 44137-2007
56.	3054 Callaghan Cove Las Cruces NM 64603	3054 Callaghan Cove Las Cruces NM 64603
57.	4957 Humperdinck Pl Racine, WI 53403	4957 Humperdickle Pl Racine, WI 53403
58.	3340 Marco Polo Pt Sandy, UT 94070-0101	3340 Marco Polo Pt Sandy, UT 94070-0010

59.	1184 Mohammed Bay Hollywood, FL 33020	1184 Mohammed Bay Hollywood, FL 33020
60.	6172 Powhaten Ave Gastonia, NC 28054	6172 Powhatten Ave Gastonia, NC 28054

Answers Address Checking - 2

1. B
2. D
3. D
4. B
5. B
6. A
7. C
8. D
9. A
10. C
11. C
12. D
13. B
14. A
15. D
16. B
17. B
18. B
19. B
20. D
21. A
22. D
23. B
24. A
25. B
26. D
27. C
28. B
29. C
30. D
31. A
32. B
33. D
34. B
35. C
36. D
37. A
38. A
39. C
40. B
41. D
42. C
43. B
44. D
45. C
46. D
47. A
48. D
49. B
50. C
51. B
52. B
53. B
54. C
55. B
56. A
57. B
58. C
59. A
60. A

Secret Key #1 - Time is Your Greatest Enemy

Pace Yourself

Wear a watch. At the beginning of the test, check the time (or start a chronometer on your watch to count the minutes), and check the time after every few questions to make sure you are "on schedule."

If you are forced to speed up, do it efficiently. Usually one or more answer choices can be eliminated without too much difficulty. Above all, don't panic. Don't speed up and just begin guessing at random choices. By pacing yourself, and continually monitoring your progress against your watch, you will always know exactly how far ahead or behind you are with your available time. If you find that you are one minute behind on the test, don't skip one question without spending any time on it, just to catch back up. Take 15 fewer seconds on the next four questions, and after four questions you'll have caught back up. Once you catch back up, you can continue working each problem at your normal pace.

Furthermore, don't dwell on the problems that you were rushed on. If a problem was taking up too much time and you made a hurried guess, it must be difficult. The difficult questions are the ones you are most likely to miss anyway, so it isn't a big loss. It is better to end with more time than you need than to run out of time.

Lastly, sometimes it is beneficial to slow down if you are constantly getting ahead of time. You are always more likely to catch a careless mistake by working more slowly than quickly, and among very high-scoring test takers (those who are likely to have lots of time left over), careless errors affect the score more than mastery of material.

Secret Key #2 - Guessing is not Guesswork

You probably know that guessing is a good idea - unlike other standardized tests, there is no penalty for getting a wrong answer. Even if you have no idea about a question, you still have a 20-25% chance of getting it right.

Most test takers do not understand the impact that proper guessing can have on their score. Unless you score extremely high, guessing will significantly contribute to your final score.

Monkeys Take the Test

What most test takers don't realize is that to insure that 20-25% chance, you have to guess randomly. If you put 20 monkeys in a room to take this test, assuming they answered once per question and behaved themselves, on average they would get 20-25% of the questions correct. Put 20 test takers in the room, and the average will be much lower among guessed questions. Why?

1. The test writers intentionally writes deceptive answer choices that "look" right. A test taker has no idea about a question, so picks the "best looking" answer, which is often wrong. The monkey has no idea what looks good and what doesn't, so will consistently be lucky about 20-25% of the time.
2. Test takers will eliminate answer choices from the guessing pool based on a hunch or intuition. Simple but correct answers often get excluded, leaving a 0% chance of being correct. The monkey has no clue, and often gets lucky with the best choice.

This is why the process of elimination endorsed by most test courses is flawed and detrimental to your performance- test takers don't guess, they make an ignorant stab in the dark that is usually worse than random.

$5 Challenge

Let me introduce one of the most valuable ideas of this course- the $5 challenge:

You only mark your "best guess" if you are willing to bet $5 on it.
You only eliminate choices from guessing if you are willing to bet $5 on it.

Why $5? Five dollars is an amount of money that is small yet not insignificant, and can really add up fast (20 questions could cost you $100). Likewise, each answer choice on one question of the test will have a small impact on your overall score, but it can really add up to a lot of points in the end.

The process of elimination IS valuable. The following shows your chance of guessing it right:

If you eliminate wrong answer choices until only this many answer choices remain:	1	2	3
Chance of getting it correct:	100%	50%	33%

However, if you accidentally eliminate the right answer or go on a hunch for an incorrect answer, your chances drop dramatically: to 0%. By guessing among all the answer choices, you are GUARANTEED to have a shot at the right answer.

That's why the $5 test is so valuable- if you give up the advantage and safety of a pure guess, it had better be worth the risk.

What we still haven't covered is how to be sure that whatever guess you make is truly random. Here's the easiest way:

Always pick the first answer choice among those remaining.

Such a technique means that you have decided, **before you see a single test question**, exactly how you are going to guess- and since the order of choices tells you nothing about which one is correct, this guessing technique is perfectly random.

This section is not meant to scare you away from making educated guesses or eliminating choices- you just need to define when a choice is worth eliminating. The $5 test, along with a pre-defined random guessing strategy, is the best way to make sure you reap all of the benefits of guessing.

Note: **Do Not guess on the address checking section.** You can make an educated guess on the Address Memory section. Due to scoring formulas you are allowed to blind guess on the Number Series and Following Oral Instructions sections. In these two sections wrong guesses do not count against you. If you do guess, go with your first choice. The first choice is usually correct. Only guess on questions as a last resort.

Secret Key #3 - Practice Smarter, Not Harder

Many test takers delay the test preparation process because they dread the awful amounts of practice time they think necessary to succeed on the test. We have refined an effective method that will take you only a fraction of the time.

There are a number of "obstacles" in your way to succeed. Among these are answering questions, finishing in time, and mastering test-taking strategies. All must be executed on the day of the test at peak performance, or your score will suffer. The test is a mental marathon that has a large impact on your future.

Just like a marathon runner, it is important to work your way up to the full challenge. So first you just worry about questions, and then time, and finally strategy:

Success Strategy

1. Find a good source for practice tests.
2. If you are willing to make a larger time investment, consider using more than one study guide- often the different approaches of multiple authors will help you "get" difficult concepts.
3. Take a practice test with no time constraints, with all study helps "open book." Take your time with questions and focus on applying strategies.
4. Take a practice test with time constraints, with all guides "open book."
5. Take a final practice test with no open material and time limits

If you have time to take more practice tests, just repeat step 5. By gradually exposing yourself to the full rigors of the test environment, you will condition your mind to the stress of test day and maximize your success.

Secret Key #4 - Prepare, Don't Procrastinate

Let me state an obvious fact: if you take the test three times, you will get three different scores. This is due to the way you feel on test day, the level of preparedness you have, and, despite the test writers' claims to the contrary, some tests WILL be easier for you than others.

Since your future depends so much on your score, you should maximize your chances of success. In order to maximize the likelihood of success, you've got to prepare in advance. This means taking practice tests and spending time learning the information and test taking strategies you will need to succeed.

Never take the test as a "practice" test, expecting that you can just take it again if you need to. Feel free to take sample tests on your own, but when you go to take the official test, be prepared, be focused, and do your best the first time!

Secret Key #5 - Test Yourself

Everyone knows that time is money. There is no need to spend too much of your time or too little of your time preparing for the test. You should only spend as much of your precious time preparing as is necessary for you to get the score you need.

Once you have taken a practice test under real conditions of time constraints, then you will know if you are ready for the test or not.

If you have scored extremely high the first time that you take the practice test, then there is not much point in spending countless hours studying. You are already there.

Benchmark your abilities by retaking practice tests and seeing how much you have improved. Once you score high enough to guarantee success, then you are ready.

If you have scored well below where you need, then knuckle down and begin studying in earnest. Check your improvement regularly through the use of practice tests under real conditions. Above all, don't worry, panic, or give up. The key is perseverance!

Then, when you go to take the test, remain confident and remember how well you did on the practice tests. If you can score high enough on a practice test, then you can do the same on the real thing.

General Strategies

The most important thing you can do is to ignore your fears and jump into the test immediately- do not be overwhelmed by any strange-sounding terms. You have to jump into the test like jumping into a pool- all at once is the easiest way.

Make Predictions

As you read and understand the question, try to guess what the answer will be. Remember that several of the answer choices are wrong, and once you begin reading them, your mind will immediately become cluttered with answer choices designed to throw you off. Your mind is typically the most focused immediately after you have read the question and digested its contents. If you can, try to predict what the correct answer will be. You may be surprised at what you can predict.

Quickly scan the choices and see if your prediction is in the listed answer choices. If it is, then you can be quite confident that you have the right answer. It still won't hurt to check the other answer choices, but most of the time, you've got it!

Answer the Question

It may seem obvious to only pick answer choices that answer the question, but the test writers can create some excellent answer choices that are wrong. Don't pick an answer just because it sounds right, or you believe it to be true. It MUST answer the question. Once you've made your selection, always go back and check it against the question and make sure that you didn't misread the question, and the answer choice does answer the question posed.

Benchmark

After you read the first answer choice, decide if you think it sounds correct or not. If it doesn't, move on to the next answer choice. If it does, mentally mark that answer choice. This doesn't mean that you've definitely selected it as your answer choice, it just means that it's the best you've seen thus far. Go ahead and read the next choice. If the next choice is worse than the one you've already selected, keep going to the next answer choice. If the next choice is better than the choice you've already selected, mentally mark the new answer choice as your best guess.

The first answer choice that you select becomes your standard. Every other answer choice must be benchmarked against that standard. That choice is correct until proven otherwise by another answer choice beating it out. Once you've decided that no other answer choice seems as good, do one final check to ensure that your answer choice answers the question posed.

Valid Information

Don't discount any of the information provided in the question. Every piece of information may be necessary to determine the correct answer. None of the information in the question is there to throw you off (while the answer choices will certainly have information to throw you off). If two seemingly unrelated topics are discussed, don't ignore either. You can be confident there is a relationship, or it wouldn't be included in the question, and you are probably going to have to determine what is that relationship to find the answer.

Avoid "Fact Traps"

Don't get distracted by a choice that is factually true. Your search is for the answer that answers the question. Stay focused and don't fall for an answer that is true but incorrect. Always go back to the question and make sure you're choosing an answer that actually answers the question and is not just a true statement. An answer can be factually correct, but it MUST answer the question asked. Additionally, two answers can both be seemingly correct, so be sure to read all of the answer choices, and make sure that you get the one that BEST answers the question.

Milk the Question

Some of the questions may throw you completely off. They might deal with a subject you have not been exposed to, or one that you haven't reviewed in years. While your lack of knowledge about the subject will be a hindrance, the question itself can give you many clues that will help you find the correct answer. Read the question carefully and look for clues. Watch particularly for adjectives and nouns describing difficult terms or words that you don't recognize. Regardless of if you completely understand a word or not, replacing it with a synonym either provided or one you more familiar with may help you to understand what the questions are asking. Rather than wracking your mind about specific detailed information concerning a difficult term or word, try to use mental substitutes that are easier to understand.

The Trap of Familiarity

Don't just choose a word because you recognize it. On difficult questions, you may not recognize a number of words in the answer choices. The test writers don't put "make-believe" words on the test; so don't think that just because you only recognize all the words in one answer choice means that answer choice must be correct. If you only recognize words in one answer choice, then focus on that one. Is it correct? Try your best to determine if it is correct. If it is, that is great, but if it doesn't, eliminate it. Each word and answer choice you eliminate increases your chances of getting the question correct, even if you then have to guess among the unfamiliar choices.

Eliminate Answers

Eliminate choices as soon as you realize they are wrong. But be careful! Make sure you consider all of the possible answer choices. Just because one appears right, doesn't mean that the next one won't be even better! The test writers will usually put more than one good answer choice for every question, so read all of them. Don't worry if you are stuck between two that seem right. By getting down to just two remaining possible choices, your odds are now 50/50. Rather than wasting too much time, play the odds. You are guessing, but guessing wisely, because you've been able to knock out some of the answer choices that you know are wrong. If you are eliminating choices and realize that the last answer choice you are left with is also obviously wrong, don't panic. Start over and consider each choice again. There may easily be something that you missed the first time and will realize on the second pass.

Tough Questions

If you are stumped on a problem or it appears too hard or too difficult, don't waste time. Move on! Remember though, if you can quickly check for obviously incorrect answer choices, your chances of guessing correctly are greatly improved. Before you completely give up, at least try to knock out a couple of possible answers. Eliminate what you can and then guess at the remaining answer choices before moving on.

Brainstorm

If you get stuck on a difficult question, spend a few seconds quickly brainstorming. Run through the complete list of possible answer choices. Look at each choice and ask yourself, "Could this answer the question satisfactorily?" Go through each answer choice and consider it independently of the other. By systematically going through all possibilities, you may find something that you would otherwise overlook. Remember that when you get stuck, it's important to try to keep moving.

Read Carefully

Understand the problem. Read the question and answer choices carefully. Don't miss the question because you misread the terms. You have plenty of time to read each question thoroughly and make sure you understand what is being asked. Yet a happy medium must be attained, so don't waste too much time. You must read carefully, but efficiently.

Face Value

When in doubt, use common sense. Always accept the situation in the problem at face value. Don't read too much into it. These problems will not require you to make huge leaps of logic. The test writers aren't trying to throw you off with a cheap trick. If you have to go beyond creativity and make a leap of logic in order to have an answer choice answer the question, then you should look at the other answer choices. Don't overcomplicate the problem by creating theoretical relationships or explanations that will warp time or space. These are normal problems rooted in reality. It's just that the applicable relationship or explanation may not be readily apparent and you have to figure things out. Use your common sense to interpret anything that isn't clear.

Prefixes

If you're having trouble with a word in the question or answer choices, try dissecting it. Take advantage of every clue that the word might include. Prefixes and suffixes can be a huge help. Usually they allow you to determine a basic meaning. Pre- means before, post- means after, pro - is positive, de- is negative. From these prefixes and suffixes, you can get an idea of the general meaning of the word and try to put it into context. Beware though of any traps. Just because con is the opposite of pro, doesn't necessarily mean congress is the opposite of progress!

Hedge Phrases

Watch out for critical "hedge" phrases, such as likely, may, can, will often, sometimes, often, almost, mostly, usually, generally, rarely, sometimes. Question writers insert these hedge phrases to cover every possibility. Often an answer choice will be wrong simply because it leaves no room for exception. Avoid answer choices that have definitive words like "exactly," and "always".

Switchback Words

Stay alert for "switchbacks". These are the words and phrases frequently used to alert you to shifts in thought. The most common switchback word is "but". Others include although, however, nevertheless, on the other hand, even though, while, in spite of, despite, regardless of.

New Information

Correct answer choices will rarely have completely new information included. Answer choices typically are straightforward reflections of the material asked about and will directly relate to the question. If a new piece of information is included in an answer choice that doesn't even seem to relate to the topic being asked about, then that answer choice is likely incorrect. All of the information needed to answer the question is usually provided for you, and so you should not have to make guesses that are unsupported or choose answer choices that require unknown information that cannot be reasoned on its own.

Time Management

On technical questions, don't get lost on the technical terms. Don't spend too much time on any one question. If you don't know what a term means, then since you don't have a dictionary, odds are you aren't going to get much further. You should immediately recognize terms as whether or not you know them. If you don't, work with the other clues that you have, the other answer choices and terms provided, but don't waste too much time trying to figure out a difficult term.

Contextual Clues

Look for contextual clues. An answer can be right but not correct. The contextual clues will help you find the answer that is most right and is correct. Understand the context in which a phrase or statement is made. This will help you make important distinctions.

Don't Panic

Panicking will not answer any questions for you. Therefore, it isn't helpful. When you first see the question, if your mind goes blank, take a deep breath. Force yourself to mechanically go through the steps of solving the problem and using the strategies you've learned.

Pace Yourself

Don't get clock fever. It's easy to be overwhelmed when you're looking at a page full of questions, your mind is full of random thoughts and feeling confused, and the clock is ticking down faster than you would like. Calm down and maintain the pace that you have set for yourself. As long as you are on track by monitoring your pace, you are guaranteed to have enough time for yourself. When you get to the last few minutes of the test, it may seem like you won't have enough time left, but if you only have as many questions as you should have left at that point, then you're right on track!

Answer Selection

The best way to pick an answer choice is to eliminate all of those that are wrong, until only one is left and confirm that is the correct answer. Sometimes though, an answer choice may immediately look right. Be careful! Take a second to make sure that the other choices are not equally obvious. Don't make a hasty mistake. There are only two times that you should stop before checking other answers. First is when you are positive that the answer choice you have selected is correct. Second is when time is almost out and you have to make a quick guess!

Check Your Work

Since you will probably not know every term listed and the answer to every question, it is important that you get credit for the ones that you do know. Don't miss any questions through careless mistakes. If at all possible, try to take a second to look back over your answer selection and make sure you've selected the correct answer choice and haven't made a costly careless mistake (such as marking an answer choice that you didn't mean to mark). This quick double check should more than pay for itself in caught mistakes for the time it costs.

Beware of Directly Quoted Answers

Sometimes an answer choice will repeat word for word a portion of the question or reference section. However, beware of such exact duplication – it may be a trap! More than likely, the correct choice will paraphrase or summarize a point, rather than being exactly the same wording.

Slang

Scientific sounding answers are better than slang ones. An answer choice that begins "To compare the outcomes…" is much more likely to be correct than one that begins "Because some people insisted…"

Extreme Statements

Avoid wild answers that throw out highly controversial ideas that are proclaimed as established fact. An answer choice that states the "process should be used in certain situations, if…" is much more likely to be correct than one that states the "process should be discontinued completely." The first is a calm rational statement and doesn't even make a definitive, uncompromising stance, using a hedge word "if" to provide wiggle room, whereas the second choice is a radical idea and far more extreme.

Answer Choice Families

When you have two or more answer choices that are direct opposites or parallels, one of them is usually the correct answer. For instance, if one answer choice states "x increases" and another answer choice states "x decreases" or "y increases," then those two or three answer choices are very similar in construction and fall into the same family of answer choices. A family of answer choices is when two or three answer choices are very similar in construction, and yet often have a directly opposite meaning. Usually the correct answer choice will be in that family of answer choices. The "odd man out" or answer choice that doesn't seem to fit the parallel construction of the other answer choices is more likely to be incorrect.

Special Report: Which Postal Exam Study Guides and Practice Tests Are Worth Your Time

We believe the following guides present uncommon value to our customers who wish to "really study" for the postal exam. While our manual teaches some valuable tricks and tips that no one else covers, learning the basic coursework tested on the postal exam is also helpful, though more time consuming.

Practice Tests

Book of US Postal Exams...
http://www.amazon.com/exec/obidos/ASIN/0931613159/actsecrets-20

This is a great source for postal exam practice tests.

Study Guide

Postal Exam Study Program...
http://www.amazon.com/exec/obidos/ASIN/0940182106/actsecrets-20

This study program is THE best comprehensive coursework guide to the postal exam. If you want to spend a couple months in preparation to squeeze every last drop out of your score, buy this book!

Special Report: I've Taken the Test, What Now?

After the test it takes three weeks to receive your test scores. A passing score is 70 percent, but those who score 95 to 100 percent are most likely to be picked for post office jobs. Obviously, not everyone who takes these tests gets a post office job and the higher you score the more chance you have of obtaining a postal job. Even if you don't get picked right away for a postal job, your test score will remain on a list of eligible persons for two years. So that means that if you don't get called right away, you may be called a few months from now or perhaps a year from now.

The list is compiled according to scores. When they reach your name on the list and call you, then you will be asked which position you prefer to apply for. If you still are interested in a postal job, you will be given a number of screenings, including a local criminal records check, drug screening, personal interview, and medical assessment.

Probably the best advice for those who are taking postal exams and applying for the postal jobs in the next month is to have patience. Applying for a postal job is not like other jobs where you send the resume, get called for an interview and get hired in two weeks. It can take months to get hired at a post office or to even hear anything from them. So if you really want to obtain a new job at the post office, don't quit your day job just yet and have patience. Because if you really want the job, your patience will pay off.

Special Report: Should the US Postal Department Manage your E-mail?

E-mail has become the dominant form of written communication for most Americans. Within direct and interactive marketing, it has become the "killer app." Spam is the growing threat to business involved in e-mail and a giant pain to all consumers who are online.

Congressional committees are sharpening knives as they prepare to create legislation that would strangle the newest marketing medium. What should be done?

The U.S. Postal Service should step into the fray. Our USPS missed the boat on e-mail and the Internet more than a decade ago. Back then, a clearer vision would have given the USPS a revenue stream as well as protect consumers from spam.

This article will not, speak to the issue of revenue per e-mail sent. The postal service has a more vital role: The controlling and issuing of permanent e-mail addresses to all U.S. households and family members.

Think about our telephone numbers. Based on where we live, we have a defined area code, a defined prefix and then four digits that are personal to the number itself. A number in Nassau County, NY, could be 516/433-1234. That number places it in Nassau County, Jericho/Syosset and then the personal numeric.

Whether the person possessing that number uses MCI, Sprint, AT&T or various other vendors, the number remains the same. It is transparent to the user or receiver as to which service is being employed.

Let the postal service do the same for e-mail and the Internet in general.

Here's how this could work:
John Doe lives at 201 Broad Stream Road, Sarasota, FL 34236-5604. The new standard e-mail for Mr. Doe would be johnd@201bsr-fl236.usa. Of course, I am sure that the postal service could devise a more creative standard than I have in this example. The ZIP+4 could be used. My point is that e-mail can be standardized by the USPS.

This has clear benefits to everyone, except the spammers, pornographers and fraudulent groups that prey through e-mail:

Each individual in a family could register with the USPS for their own address. At the Doe household, Mary, John Jr. and Peter all can have their own e-mail addresses.

Plus, for an "upcharge," they can have a family Web site: www.201bsr-fl236.usa, to which each member could add a personal page.

Each household or e-mail address could simply block non-USPS URLs from their e-mail bin. By simply using the filter on their e-mail program, offshore spam would be eliminated.

It would allow the USPS Inspection Service and other federal agencies to pursue domestic e-mail abusers.
It would let households and individuals change service providers yet keep their e-mail addresses.

Marketers could target geographically and use all the methodology of traditional direct marketing. This in itself would make e-mails more relevant to the recipient and response margins and ROI more profitable.
Remove requests would be honored through traditional suppression methods.

Change of address and new e-mail addresses would be combined to allow for greater efficiencies to all concerned.

Businesses would have a choice, either the above standard e-mail or one that maintained their individual corporate URL.

For all government business, consumers and business alike would be required to use the standard postal e-mail address. Therefore, IRS communications and filings as well as banking and secure transactions with SEC institutions would be through the system.

Who would lose? Excluding the bad guys, the ISPs such as AOL, Earthlink and others stand to lose their branding via the URL of the e-mail address. This is a small price to end the blight of spam and add the benefits to consumers and marketers alike.

Furthermore, it lets the USPS become a source of renewed energy and services that will come from an agency that has been around since the beginning of the republic.

Globalization of legitimate e-mails from other countries can be combined into this program, once again through the postal service. Discussions of this type of scenario are taking place. Lobbyists for different interests are not in favor of this program.

We should think about this or other consumer-oriented e-mail programs that will let the medium survive.

Special Report: Postal Mailing Technicalities

Addressing Your Mail

The accuracy of the address affects the speed and handling of your mail.

Return Address

Print or type your address in the upper left corner on the front of the envelope.

Extra Services

Place labels for extra services, such as Certified Mail, to the left of the postage.

Postage

Use a stamp, postage meter, or PC Postage to affix the correct amount.

Street Address

Use a post office box or street address, but not both. If the address also has a directional (for instance, "NW " for Northwest), be sure to use it. There may be more than one Main Street.

Apartment or Suite Number

The correct apartment or suite number helps to ensure delivery to the right location.

City, State, and ZIP Code

To find the correct spelling of a city name or to find a ZIP Code, visit www.usps.com or call 1-800-ASK-USPS. Using the correct ZIP Code helps to direct your mail more efficiently and accurately.

Envelopes

Letters, bills, greeting cards, and other documents can be sent in standard white, manila, or recycled paper envelopes. Items needing extra protection can be sent in bubble-lined, padded paper, or waterproof envelopes. These envelopes, along with stationery and prepaid First-Class Mail postcards and envelopes, can be purchased at the Post Office.

Express Mail and Priority Mail envelopes of various sizes are available free of charge at your Post Office for items sent using either of these services. While you are not required to use the free envelopes, you must use the address label provided for Express Mail.

Address Placement

Print the delivery and return addresses on the same side of your envelope or card. The addresses should be written parallel to the longest side.

Addressing Letters

Print or type clearly with a pen or permanent marker so the address is legible from an arm's length away. Do not use commas or periods.

Return Address

A return address helps return the mail to you if it is undeliverable.

Express Mail®

For Express Mail, you must use the free address labels provided by the Post Office.

Military Mail

Military addresses must show the grade, full name with middle name or initial, and PSC number, unit number, or ship name. Replace the city name with "APO " or "FPO," and the state with "AA," "AE," or "AP," and use a special ZIP Code.

Abbreviations

A list of commonly used state, street, and other abbreviations is available online.

Preparing Packages

Careful preparation of your package helps to ensure safe delivery.

The Box

Choose a box with enough room for cushioning material around the contents. Sturdy paperboard or corrugated fiberboard boxes are best for weights up to 10 pounds. If you are reusing a box, cover all previous labels and markings with heavy black marker or adhesive labels.

Where to Find Boxes

You can purchase boxes and tubes of various sizes at most Post Offices. Express Mail and Priority Mail boxes and tubes are available for free at the Post Office for items sent using either of these services. While you are not required to use the free packaging for these services, you must use the address label provided by the Post Office for Express Mail. To order 10-packs or large quantities of Express Mail or Priority Mail boxes or tubes at no extra charge, call 1·800·222·1811 or visit http://supplies.usps.gov.

Cushioning

Place the cushioning all around your item or items. You can use newspaper, styrofoam "peanuts," bubble wrap, or shredded paper. Close and shake the box to see if you have enough cushioning. If you hear items shifting, add more cushioning.

Placing an extra address label with the delivery and return addresses inside the package will ensure that the item can be delivered in case the outside label becomes damaged or falls off.

Mailing Fragile Items

Use foamed plastic or padding to protect your items, placing the cushioning inside hollow items as well. Careful packaging is the best way to safeguard your valuable items against damage.

Mailing Heavy Items

If you are mailing a very heavy or very dense item, start with a sturdy box, pack the contents securely with a strong material for bracing to prevent shifting, and tape all the edges with reinforced tape. Packages heavier than 70 pounds cannot be mailed.

Sealing

Tape the opening of your box and reinforce all seams with 2 inch wide tape. Use clear or brown packaging tape, reinforced packing tape, or paper tape. Do not use cord, string, or twine because they can get caught in mail processing equipment. Place a strip of clear packaging tape over your label to prevent the address from smearing.

Return Address

Print or type your address in the upper left corner on the same side of the package as the delivery address.

Special Report: Sending and Receiving Mail

Here are some useful mailing hints for senders and recipients.

Sending Mail

You can send mail by:

Dropping it into a blue collection box
Leaving it in your home mailbox
Bringing it to a Post Office
Packages that weigh one pound or more must be handed to your letter carrier or taken to a Post Office. Many locations are open late and on weekends.

Scheduling a Pickup

For a fee of $12.50, a letter carrier will make a special trip to your home to pick up Priority Mail, Express Mail, or Parcel Post packages that have postage affixed. There is no additional charge for picking up multiple pieces of mail. Visit www.usps.com or call 1·800·222·1811 for additional information or to schedule a pickup.

Holding Mail

If you are going to be away from home, you may want to temporarily stop delivery of your mail. To hold your mail, visit www.usps.com, call 1·800·ASK·USPS, or fill out PS Form 8076 Authorization to Hold Mail available online or at the Post Office. When you return, you can either pick up your mail from the Post Office or have it delivered to your home.

Change of Address and Mail Forwarding

Before you move, get a copy of the Mover's Guide from your Post Office and return the completed form to your letter carrier or your Post Office. The Mover's Guide includes postcards to help you contact banks, utility companies, and magazine publishers with your new address. You can also complete a change of address application online.

Notify your Post Office at least one month before you move to ensure uninterrupted mail service. All Express Mail, Priority Mail, and First-Class Mail will be forwarded at no charge for one year. Magazines and newspapers will be forwarded for 60 days.

Signing for Mail

Some pieces of mail require a signature from the recipient at the time of delivery. This includes items sent with Express Mail, Certified Mail, COD, Insured Mail, Registered Mail, Return Receipt, and Signature Confirmation.

Recipient Responsibilities

When you sign for a piece of mail, you acknowledge delivery. The Postal Service's liability ends when you sign for the mail. You may ask the letter carrier for the sender's name and address before you accept the mail. You may not open the mail, but you may look at it as long as the letter carrier is holding it before you choose to sign for it.

Delivery If Recipient Is Not Home

If no one is home when the letter carrier attempts delivery, the letter carrier will leave a notice and return the item to the Post Office. Check the notice for specific instructions or call 1call 1·800·222·1811 to have the mail redelivered. If the sender has not asked for Restricted Delivery, the carrier may deliver the mail to anyone who receives mail at that address.

Confirming Delivery

Visit www.usps.com or call 1·800·222·1811 to get delivery information on Express Mail and mail with extra services. You will need the item number from your mailing receipt or label.

Restricting Delivery

Restricted Delivery service ensures that only a specified person (or the person's authorized agent) will receive a piece of mail. This service costs $3.50. Restricted Delivery is only available if you also purchase Certified Mail, Insured Mail (for more than $50 coverage), or Registered Mail.

Filing a Claim

You can file a claim for compensation for loss or damage of Insured Mail, Registered Mail, and Express Mail. Take the damaged item and proof of its value along with the original box and packaging materials to your Post Office. A clerk will help you file your claim.

Perishable Items

Some items require special packaging or special permission to be mailed. Call 1·800·ASK·USPS or visit your Post Office to find out how to mail these items:

Live animals
Fresh fruits and vegetables
Plants

Special Report: Postal Products and Services

For more information about these services, visit www.usps.com, call 1·800·ASK·USPS, or stop by your Post Office.

International Mail

You can mail letters, large envelopes, and packages from the United States to other countries. As with domestic mail, you can choose the best service based on speed, cost, and extra services. To learn more about options for international mail and to calculate postage, visit www.uspsglobal.com or call 1·800·ASK·USPS. Your Post Office can also help you send mail internationally.

Military Mail

The Postal Service can deliver your letters and packages to more than 300 military Post Offices overseas. Many services available for domestic mail are also available for military mail. There may be restrictions on the size or content of your mail. Call 1·800·ASK·USPS for details.

Money Orders

Money orders are a safe alternative to sending cash through the mail. A lost or stolen money order can be replaced. You can buy money orders at all Post Offices in amounts up to $1,000 each. Most money orders cost $0.90-$1.25.

Net.Post® Personal Services

You can combine the ease and speed of the internet with the power of hard copy mail. Use Net.Post Services to create and send postcards, letters, greeting cards, and newsletters conveniently from your home computer. Simply upload your documents or choose a design from the gallery, input one or more addresses, pay with a credit card, and the Postal Service does the rest. Everyone loves to receive mail, and this is an easy way to keep in touch.

Passports

Some Post Offices offer passport application and renewal services. For more information about passport application forms and locations, call 1·800·ASK·USPS or visit http://travel.state.gov.

Paying for Merchandise

For a small fee, you can send merchandise COD (Collect on Delivery) and have the Postal Service collect payment from the recipient and send it to you. If you buy and sell merchandise over the internet, Pay@Delivery combines an electronic payment service with Delivery Confirmation.

PC Postage™

Enjoy the convenience of printing postage directly from your home or office using PC Postage products. Postal Service-approved vendors offer hardware and software products that allow you to purchase and print postage using a computer and the internet. Learn more at www.usps.com/postagesolutions.

Post Office™ Boxes

A post office box is a great way to receive mail where and when it's most convenient for you. You can get a P.O. box at most Post Offices. Prices vary depending on the location of the Post Office and the P.O. box size.

Stamp Collecting

If you are interested in stamp collecting or the U.S. Philatelic Magazine, visit www.usps.com or call 1·800·STAMP24. Stamp products, such as mugs and t-shirts, make great gifts.

Special Report: What Your Test Score Will Tell You About Your IQ

Did you know that most standardized tests correlate very strongly with IQ? In fact, your general intelligence is a better predictor of your success than any other factor, and most tests intentionally measure this trait to some degree to ensure that those selected by the test are truly qualified for the test's purposes.

Before we can delve into the relation between your test score and IQ, I will first have to explain what exactly is IQ. Here's the formula:

Your IQ = 100 + (Number of standard deviations below or above the average)*15

Now, let's define standard deviations by using an example. If we have 5 people with 5 different heights, then first we calculate the average. Let's say the average was 65 inches. The standard deviation is the "average distance" away from the average of each of the members. It is a direct measure of variability - if the 5 people included Jackie Chan and Shaquille O'Neal, obviously there's a lot more variability in that group than a group of 5 sisters who are all within 6 inches in height of each other. The standard deviation uses a number to characterize the average range of difference within a group.

A convenient feature of most groups is that they have a "normal" distribution- makes sense that most things would be normal, right? Without getting into a bunch of statistical mumbo-jumbo, you just need to know that if you know the average of the group and the standard deviation, you can successfully predict someone's percentile rank in the group.

Confused? Let me give you an example. If instead of 5 people's heights, we had 100 people, we could figure out their rank in height JUST by knowing the average, standard deviation, and their height. We wouldn't need to know each person's height and manually rank them, we could just predict their rank based on three numbers.

What this means is that you can take your PERCENTILE rank that is often given with your test and relate this to your RELATIVE IQ of people taking the test - that is, your IQ relative to the people taking the test. Obviously, there's no way to know your actual IQ because the people taking a standardized test are usually not very good samples of the general population- many of those with extremely low IQ's never achieve a level of success or competency necessary to complete a typical standardized test. In fact, professional psychologists who measure IQ actually have to use non-written tests that can fairly measure the IQ of those not able to complete a traditional test.

The bottom line is to not take your test score too seriously, but it is fun to compute your "relative IQ" among the people who took the test with you. I've done the calculations below. Just look up your percentile rank in the left and then you'll see your "relative IQ" for your test in the right hand column-

Percentile Rank	Your Relative IQ		Percentile Rank	Your Relative IQ
99	135		59	103
98	131		58	103
97	128		57	103
96	126		56	102
95	125		55	102
94	123		54	102
93	122		53	101
92	121		52	101
91	120		51	100
90	119		50	100
89	118		49	100
88	118		48	99
87	117		47	99
86	116		46	98
85	116		45	98
84	115		44	98
83	114		43	97
82	114		42	97
81	113		41	97
80	113		40	96
79	112		39	96
78	112		38	95
77	111		37	95
76	111		36	95
75	110		35	94
74	110		34	94
73	109		33	93
72	109		32	93
71	108		31	93
70	108		30	92
69	107		29	92
68	107		28	91
67	107		27	91
66	106		26	90
65	106		25	90
64	105		24	89
63	105		23	89
62	105		22	88
61	104		21	88
60	104		20	87

Special Report: Retaking the Test: What Are Your Chances at Improving Your Score?

After going through the experience of taking a major test, many test takers feel that once is enough. The test usually comes during a period of transition in the test taker's life, and taking the test is only one of a series of important events. With so many distractions and conflicting recommendations, it may be difficult for a test taker to rationally determine whether or not he should retake the test after viewing his scores.

The importance of the test usually only adds to the burden of the retake decision. However, don't be swayed by emotion. There a few simple questions that you can ask yourself to guide you as you try to determine whether a retake would improve your score:

1. What went wrong? Why wasn't your score what you expected?

Can you point to a single factor or problem that you feel caused the low score? Were you sick on test day? Was there an emotional upheaval in your life that caused a distraction? Were you late for the test or not able to use the full time allotment? If you can point to any of these specific, individual problems, then a retake should definitely be considered.

2. Is there enough time to improve?

Many problems that may show up in your score report may take a lot of time for improvement. A deficiency in a particular math skill may require weeks or months of tutoring and studying to improve. If you have enough time to improve an identified weakness, then a retake should definitely be considered.

3. How will additional scores be used? Will a score average, highest score, or most recent score be used?

Different test scores may be handled completely differently. If you've taken the test multiple times, sometimes your highest score is used, sometimes your average score is computed and used, and sometimes your most recent score is used. Make sure you understand what method will be used to evaluate your scores, and use that to help you determine whether a retake should be considered.

4. Are my practice test scores significantly higher than my actual test score?

If you have taken a lot of practice tests and are consistently scoring at a much higher level than your actual test score, then you should consider a retake. However, if you've taken five practice tests and only one of your scores was higher than your actual test score, or if your practice test scores were only slightly higher than your actual test score, then it is unlikely that you will significantly increase your score.

5. Do I need perfect scores or will I be able to live with this score? Will this score still allow me to follow my dreams?

What kind of score is acceptable to you? Is your current score "good enough?" Do you have to have a certain score in order to pursue the future of your dreams? If you won't be happy with your current score, and there's no way that you could live with it, then you should consider a retake. However, don't get your hopes up. If you are looking for significant improvement, that may or may not be possible. But if you won't be happy otherwise, it is at least worth the effort.

Remember that there are other considerations. To achieve your dream, it is likely that your grades may also be taken into account. A great test score is usually not the only thing necessary to succeed. Make sure that you aren't overemphasizing the importance of a high test score.

Furthermore, a retake does not always result in a higher score. Some test takers will score lower on a retake, rather than higher. One study shows that one-fourth of test takers will achieve a significant improvement in test score, while one-sixth of test takers will actually show a decrease. While this shows that most test takers will improve, the majority will only improve their scores a little and a retake may not be worth the test taker's effort.

Finally, if a test is taken only once and is considered in the added context of good grades on the part of a test taker, the person reviewing the grades and scores may be tempted to assume that the test taker just had a bad day while taking the test, and may discount the low test score in favor of the high grades. But if the test is retaken and the scores are approximately the same, then the validity of the low scores are only confirmed. Therefore, a retake could actually hurt a test taker by definitely bracketing a test taker's score ability to a limited range.

Special Report: What is Test Anxiety and How to Overcome It?

The very nature of tests caters to some level of anxiety, nervousness or tension, just as we feel for any important event that occurs in our lives. A little bit of anxiety or nervousness can be a good thing. It helps us with motivation, and makes achievement just that much sweeter. However, too much anxiety can be a problem; especially if it hinders our ability to function and perform.

"Test anxiety," is the term that refers to the emotional reactions that some test-takers experience when faced with a test or exam. Having a fear of testing and exams is based upon a rational fear, since the test-taker's performance can shape the course of an academic career. Nevertheless, experiencing excessive fear of examinations will only interfere with the test-takers ability to perform, and his/her chances to be successful.

There are a large variety of causes that can contribute to the development and sensation of test anxiety. These include, but are not limited to lack of performance and worrying about issues surrounding the test.

Lack of Preparation

Lack of preparation can be identified by the following behaviors or situations:

Not scheduling enough time to study, and therefore cramming the night before the test or exam

Managing time poorly, to create the sensation that there is not enough time to do everything

Failing to organize the text information in advance, so that the study material consists of the entire text and not simply the pertinent information
Poor overall studying habits

Worrying, on the other hand, can be related to both the test taker, or many other factors around him/her that will be affected by the results of the test. These include worrying about:

Previous performances on similar exams, or exams in general
How friends and other students are achieving
The negative consequences that will result from a poor grade or failure

There are three primary elements to test anxiety. Physical components, which involve the same typical bodily reactions as those to acute anxiety (to be discussed below). Emotional factors have to do with fear or panic. Mental or cognitive issues concerning attention spans and memory abilities.

Physical Signals

There are many different symptoms of test anxiety, and these are not limited to mental and emotional strain. Frequently there are a range of physical signals that will let a test taker know that he/she is suffering from test anxiety. These bodily changes can include the following:

Perspiring
Sweaty palms
Wet, trembling hands
Nausea
Dry mouth
A knot in the stomach

Headache

Faintness

Muscle tension

Aching shoulders, back and neck

Rapid heart beat

Feeling too hot/cold

To recognize the sensation of test anxiety, a test-taker should monitor him/herself for the following sensations:

The physical distress symptoms as listed above

Emotional sensitivity, expressing emotional feelings such as the need to cry or laugh too much, or a sensation of anger or helplessness

A decreased ability to think, causing the test-taker to blank out or have racing thoughts that are hard to organize or control.

Though most students will feel some level of anxiety when faced with a test or exam, the majority can cope with that anxiety and maintain it at a manageable level. However, those who cannot are faced with a very real and very serious condition, which can and should be controlled for the immeasurable benefit of this sufferer.

Naturally, these sensations lead to negative results for the testing experience. The most common effects of test anxiety have to do with nervousness and mental blocking.

Nervousness

Nervousness can appear in several different levels:

The test-taker's difficulty, or even inability to read and understand the questions on the test
The difficulty or inability to organize thoughts to a coherent form
The difficulty or inability to recall key words and concepts relating to the testing questions (especially essays)
The receipt of poor grades on a test, though the test material was well known by the test taker

Conversely, a person may also experience mental blocking, which involves:

Blanking out on test questions
Only remembering the correct answers to the questions when the test has already finished.

Fortunately for test anxiety sufferers, beating these feelings, to a large degree, has to do with proper preparation. When a test taker has a feeling of preparedness, then anxiety will be dramatically lessened.

The first step to resolving anxiety issues is to distinguish which of the two types of anxiety are being suffered. If the anxiety is a direct result of a lack of preparation, this should be considered a normal reaction, and the anxiety level (as opposed to the test results) shouldn't be anything to worry about. However, if, when adequately prepared, the test-taker still panics, blanks out, or seems to overreact, this is not a fully rational reaction. While this can be considered normal too, there are many ways to combat and overcome these effects.

Remember that anxiety cannot be entirely eliminated, however, there are ways to minimize it, to make the anxiety easier to manage. Preparation is one of the best ways to minimize test anxiety. Therefore the following techniques are wise in order to best fight off any anxiety that may want to build.

To begin with, try to avoid cramming before a test, whenever it is possible. By trying to memorize an entire term's worth of information in one day, you'll be shocking your system, and not giving yourself a very good chance to absorb the information. This is an easy path to anxiety, so for those who suffer from test anxiety, cramming should not even be considered an option.

Instead of cramming, work throughout the semester to combine all of the material which is presented throughout the semester, and work on it gradually as the course goes by, making sure to master the main concepts first, leaving minor details for a week or so before the test.

To study for the upcoming exam, be sure to pose questions that may be on the examination, to gauge the ability to answer them by integrating the ideas from your texts, notes and lectures, as well as any supplementary readings.

If it is truly impossible to cover all of the information that was covered in that particular term, concentrate on the most important portions, that can be covered very well. Learn these concepts as best as possible, so that when the test comes, a goal can be made to use these concepts as presentations of your knowledge.

In addition to study habits, changes in attitude are critical to beating a struggle with test anxiety. In fact, an improvement of the perspective over the entire test-taking experience can actually help a test taker to enjoy studying and therefore improve the overall experience. Be certain not to overemphasize the significance of the grade - know that the result of the test is neither a reflection of self worth, nor is it a measure of intelligence; one grade will not predict a person's future success.

To improve an overall testing outlook, the following steps should be tried:

Keeping in mind that the most reasonable expectation for taking a test is to expect to try to demonstrate as much of what you know as you possibly can.
Reminding ourselves that a test is only one test; this is not the only one, and there will be others.
The thought of thinking of oneself in an irrational, all-or-nothing term should be avoided at all costs.
A reward should be designated for after the test, so there's something to look forward to. Whether it be going to a movie, going out to eat, or simply visiting friends, schedule it in advance, and do it no matter what result is expected on the exam.

Test-takers should also keep in mind that the basics are some of the most important things, even beyond anti-anxiety techniques and studying. Never neglect the basic social, emotional and biological needs, in order to try to absorb information. In order to best achieve, these three factors must be held as just as important as the studying itself.

Study Steps

Remember the following important steps for studying:

Maintain healthy nutrition and exercise habits. Continue both your recreational activities and social pass times. These both contribute to your physical and emotional well being.

Be certain to get a good amount of sleep, especially the night before the test, because when you're overtired you are not able to perform to the best of your best ability.
Keep the studying pace to a moderate level by taking breaks when they are needed, and varying the work whenever possible, to keep the mind fresh instead of getting bored.
When enough studying has been done that all the material that can be learned has been learned, and the test taker is prepared for the test, stop studying and do something relaxing such as listening to music, watching a movie, or taking a warm bubble bath.

There are also many other techniques to minimize the uneasiness or apprehension that is experienced along with test anxiety before, during, or even after the examination. In fact, there are a great deal of things that can be done to stop anxiety from interfering with lifestyle and performance. Again, remember that anxiety will not be eliminated entirely, and it shouldn't be. Otherwise that "up" feeling for exams would not exist, and most of us depend on that sensation to perform better than usual. However, this anxiety has to be at a level that is manageable.

Of course, as we have just discussed, being prepared for the exam is half the battle right away. Attending all classes, finding out what knowledge will be expected on the exam, and knowing the exam schedules are easy steps to lowering anxiety. Keeping up with work will remove the need to cram, and efficient study habits will eliminate wasted time. Studying should be done in an ideal location for concentration, so that it is simple to become interested in the material and give it complete attention. A method such as SQ3R (Survey, Question, Read, Recite, Review) is a wonderful key to follow to make sure that the study habits are as effective as possible, especially in the case of learning from a textbook. Flashcards are great techniques for memorization. Learning to take good notes will mean that notes will be full of useful information, so that less sifting will need to be done to seek out what is pertinent for studying. Reviewing notes after class and then again on occasion will keep the information fresh in the mind. From notes that have been taken summary sheets and outlines can be made for simpler reviewing.

A study group can also be a very motivational and helpful place to study, as there will be a sharing of ideas, all of the minds can work together, to make sure that everyone understands, and the studying will be made more interesting because it will be a social occasion.

Basically, though, as long as the test-taker remains organized and self confident, with efficient study habits, less time will need to be spent studying, and higher grades will be achieved.

To become self confident, there are many useful steps. The first of these is "self talk." It has been shown through extensive research, that self-talk for students who suffer from test anxiety, should be well monitored, in order to make sure that it contributes to self confidence as opposed to sinking the student. Frequently the self talk of test-anxious students is negative or self-defeating, thinking that everyone else is smarter and faster, that they always mess up, and that if they don't do well, they'll fail the entire course. It is important to decreasing anxiety that awareness is made of self talk. Try writing any negative self thoughts and then disputing them with a positive statement instead. Begin self-encouragement as though it was a friend speaking. Repeat positive statements to help reprogram the mind to believing in successes instead of failures.

Helpful Techniques

Other extremely helpful techniques include:

Self-visualization of doing well and reaching goals
While aiming for an "A" level of understanding, don't try to "overprotect" by setting your expectations lower. This will only convince the mind to stop studying in order to meet the lower expectations.
Don't make comparisons with the results or habits of other students. These are individual factors, and different things work for different people, causing different results.
Strive to become an expert in learning what works well, and what can be done in order to improve. Consider collecting this data in a journal.
Create rewards for after studying instead of doing things before studying that will only turn into avoidance behaviors.
Make a practice of relaxing - by using methods such as progressive relaxation, self-hypnosis, guided imagery, etc - in order to make relaxation an automatic sensation.
Work on creating a state of relaxed concentration so that concentrating will take on the focus of the mind, so that none will be wasted on worrying.
Take good care of the physical self by eating well and getting enough sleep.
Plan in time for exercise and stick to this plan.

Beyond these techniques, there are other methods to be used before, during and after the test that will help the test-taker perform well in addition to overcoming anxiety.

Before the exam comes the academic preparation. This involves establishing a study schedule and beginning at least one week before the actual date of the test. By doing this, the anxiety of not having enough time to study for the test will be automatically eliminated. Moreover, this will make the studying a much more effective experience, ensuring that the learning will be an easier process. This relieves much undue pressure on the test-taker.

Summary sheets, note cards, and flash cards with the main concepts and examples of these main concepts should be prepared in advance of the actual studying time. A topic should never be eliminated from this process. By omitting a topic because it isn't expected to be on the test is only setting up the test-taker for anxiety should it actually appear on the exam. Utilize the course syllabus for laying out the topics that should be studied. Carefully go over the notes that were made in class, paying special attention to any of the issues that the professor took special care to emphasize while lecturing in class. In the textbooks, use the chapter review, or if possible, the chapter tests, to begin your review.

It may even be possible to ask the instructor what information will be covered on the exam, or what the format of the exam will be (for example, multiple choice, essay, free form, true-false). Additionally, see if it is possible to find out how many questions will be on the test. If a review sheet or sample test has been offered by the professor, make good use of it, above anything else, for the preparation for the test. Another great resource for getting to know the examination is reviewing tests from previous semesters. Use these tests to review, and aim to achieve a 100% score on each of the possible topics. With a few exceptions, the goal that you set for yourself is the highest one that you will reach.

Take all of the questions that were assigned as homework, and rework them to any other possible course material. The more problems reworked, the more skill and confidence will form as a result. When forming the solution to a problem, write out each of the steps. Don't simply do head work. By doing as many steps on paper as possible, much clarification and therefore confidence will be formed. Do this with as many homework problems as possible, before checking the answers. By checking the answer after each problem, a reinforcement will exist, that will not be on the exam. Study situations should be as exam-like as possible, to prime the test-taker's system for the experience. By waiting to check the answers at the end, a psychological advantage will be formed, to decrease the stress factor.

Another fantastic reason for not cramming is the avoidance of confusion in concepts, especially when it comes to mathematics. 8-10 hours of study will become one hundred percent more effective if it is spread out over a week or at least several days, instead of doing it all in one sitting. Recognize that the human brain requires time in order to assimilate new material, so frequent breaks and a span of study time over several days will be much more beneficial.

Additionally, don't study right up until the point of the exam. Studying should stop a minimum of one hour before the exam begins. This allows the brain to rest and put things in their proper order. This will also provide the time to become as relaxed as possible when going into the examination room. The test-taker will also have time to eat well and eat sensibly. Know that the brain needs food as much as the rest of the body. With enough food and enough sleep, as well as a relaxed attitude, the body and the mind are primed for success.

Avoid any anxious classmates who are talking about the exam. These students only spread anxiety, and are not worth sharing the anxious sentimentalities.

Before the test also involves creating a positive attitude, so mental preparation should also be a point of concentration. There are many keys to creating a positive attitude. Should fears become rushing in, make a visualization of taking the exam, doing well, and seeing an A written on the paper. Write out a list of affirmations that will bring a feeling of confidence, such as "I am doing well in my English class," "I studied well and know my material," "I enjoy this class." Even if the affirmations aren't believed at first, it sends a positive message to the subconscious which will result in an alteration of the overall belief system, which is the system that creates reality.

If a sensation of panic begins, work with the fear and imagine the very worst! Work through the entire scenario of not passing the test, failing the entire course, and dropping out of school, followed by not getting a job, and pushing a shopping cart through the dark alley where you'll live. This will place things into perspective! Then, practice deep breathing and create a visualization of the opposite situation - achieving an "A" on the exam, passing the entire course, receiving the degree at a graduation ceremony.

On the day of the test, there are many things to be done to ensure the best results, as well as the most calm outlook. The following stages are suggested in order to maximize test-taking potential:

Begin the examination day with a moderate breakfast, and avoid any coffee or beverages with caffeine if the test taker is prone to jitters. Even people who are used to managing caffeine can feel jittery or light-headed when it is taken on a test day.

Attempt to do something that is relaxing before the examination begins. As last minute cramming clouds the mastering of overall concepts, it is better to use this time to create a calming outlook.

Be certain to arrive at the test location well in advance, in order to provide time to select a location that is away from doors, windows and other distractions, as well as giving enough time to relax before the test begins.

Keep away from anxiety generating classmates who will upset the sensation of stability and relaxation that is being attempted before the exam.

Should the waiting period before the exam begins cause anxiety, create a self-distraction by reading a light magazine or something else that is relaxing and simple.

During the exam itself, read the entire exam from beginning to end, and find out how much time should be allotted to each individual problem. Once writing the exam, should more time be taken for a problem, it should be abandoned, in order to begin another problem. If there is time at the end, the unfinished problem can always be returned to and completed.

Read the instructions very carefully - twice - so that unpleasant surprises won't follow during or after the exam has ended.

When writing the exam, pretend that the situation is actually simply the completion of homework within a library, or at home. This will assist in forming a relaxed atmosphere, and will allow the brain extra focus for the complex thinking function.

Begin the exam with all of the questions with which the most confidence is felt. This will build the confidence level regarding the entire exam and will begin a quality momentum. This will also create encouragement for trying the problems where uncertainty resides.

Going with the "gut instinct" is always the way to go when solving a problem. Second guessing should be avoided at all costs. Have confidence in the ability to do well.

For essay questions, create an outline in advance that will keep the mind organized and make certain that all of the points are remembered. For multiple choice, read every answer, even if the correct one has been spotted - a better one may exist.

Continue at a pace that is reasonable and not rushed, in order to be able to work carefully. Provide enough time to go over the answers at the end, to check for small errors that can be corrected.

Should a feeling of panic begin, breathe deeply, and think of the feeling of the body releasing sand through its pores. Visualize a calm, peaceful place, and include all of the sights, sounds and sensations of this image. Continue the deep breathing, and take a few minutes to continue this with closed eyes. When all is well again, return to the test.

If a "blanking" occurs for a certain question, skip it and move on to the next question. There will be time to return to the other question later. Get everything done that can be done, first, to guarantee all the grades that can be compiled, and to build all of the confidence possible. Then return to the weaker questions to build the marks from there.

Remember, one's own reality can be created, so as long as the belief is there, success will follow. And remember: anxiety can happen later, right now, there's an exam to be written!

After the examination is complete, whether there is a feeling for a good grade or a bad grade, don't dwell on the exam, and be certain to follow through on the reward that was promised...and enjoy it! Don't dwell on any mistakes that have been made, as there is nothing that can be done at this point anyway.

Additionally, don't begin to study for the next test right away. Do something relaxing for a while, and let the mind relax and prepare itself to begin absorbing information again.

From the results of the exam - both the grade and the entire experience, be certain to learn from what has gone on. Perfect studying habits and work some more on confidence in order to make the next examination experience even better than the last one.

Learn to avoid places where openings occurred for laziness, procrastination and day dreaming.

Use the time between this exam and the next one to better learn to relax, even learning to relax on cue, so that any anxiety can be controlled during the next exam. Learn how to relax the body. Slouch in your chair if that helps. Tighten and then relax all of the different muscle groups, one group at a time, beginning with the feet and then working all the way up to the neck and face. This will ultimately relax the muscles more than they were to begin with. Learn how to breathe deeply and comfortably, and focus on this breathing going in and out as a relaxing thought. With every exhale, repeat the word "relax."

As common as test anxiety is, it is very possible to overcome it. Make yourself one of the test-takers who overcome this frustrating hindrance.

Special Report: How to Overcome Your Fear of Math

If this article started by saying "Math," many of us would feel a shiver crawl up our spines, just by reading that simple word. Images of torturous years in those crippling desks of the math classes can become so vivid to our consciousness that we can almost smell those musty textbooks, and see the smudges of the #2 pencils on our fingers.

If you are still a student, feeling the impact of these sometimes overwhelming classroom sensations, you are not alone if you get anxious at just the thought of taking that compulsory math course. Does your heart beat just that much faster when you have to split the bill for lunch among your friends with a group of your friends? Do you truly believe that you simply don't have the brain for math? Certainly you're good at other things, but math just simply isn't one of them? Have you ever avoided activities, or other school courses because they appear to involve mathematics, with which you're simply not comfortable?

If any one or more of these "symptoms" can be applied to you, you could very well be suffering from a very real condition called "Math Anxiety."

It's not at all uncommon for people to think that they have some sort of math disability or allergy, when in actuality, their block is a direct result of the way in which they were taught math!

In the late 1950's with the dawning of the space age, New Math - a new "fuzzy math" reform that focuses on higher-order thinking, conceptual understanding and solving problems - took the country by storm. It's now becoming ever more clear that teachers were not supplied with the correct, practical and effective way in which they should be teaching new math so that students will understand the methods comfortably. So is it any wonder that so many students struggled so deeply, when their teachers were required to change their entire math systems without the foundation of proper training? Even if you have not been personally, directly affected by that precise event, its impact is still as rampant as ever.

Basically, the math teachers of today are either the teachers who began teaching the new math in the first place (without proper training) or they are the students of the math teachers who taught new math without proper training. Therefore, unless they had a unique, exceptional teacher, their primary, consistent examples of teaching math have been teachers using methods that are not conducive to the general understanding of the entire class. This explains why your discomfort (or fear) of math is not at all rare.

It is very clear why being called up to the chalk board to solve a math problem is such a common example of a terrifying situation for students - and it has very little to do with a fear of being in front of the class. Most of us have had a minimum of one humiliating experience while standing with chalk dusted fingers, with the eyes of every math student piercing through us. These are the images that haunt us all the way through adulthood. But it does not mean that we cannot learn math. It just means that we could be developing a solid case of math anxiety.

But what exactly is math anxiety? It's an very strong emotional sensation of anxiety, panic, or fear that people feel when they think about or must apply their ability to understand mathematics. Sufferers of math anxiety frequently believe that they are incapable of doing activities or taking classes that involve math skills. In fact, some people with math anxiety have developed such a fear that it has become a phobia; aptly named math phobia.

The incidence of math anxiety, especially among college students, but also among high school students, has risen considerably over the last 10 years, and currently this increase shows no signs of slowing down. Frequently students will even chose their college majors and programs based specifically on how little math will be compulsory for the completion of the degree.

The prevalence of math anxiety has become so dramatic on college campuses that many of these schools have special counseling programs that are designed to assist math anxious students to deal with their discomfort and their math problems.

Math anxiety itself is not an intellectual problem, as many people have been lead to believe; it is, in fact, an emotional problem that stems from improper math teaching techniques that have slowly built and reinforced these feelings. However, math anxiety can result in an intellectual problem when its symptoms interfere with a person's ability to learn and understand math.

The fear of math can cause a sort of "glitch" in the brain that can cause an otherwise clever person to stumble over even the simplest of math problems. A study by Dr. Mark H. Ashcraft of Cleveland State University in Ohio showed that college students who usually perform well, but who suffer from math anxiety, will suffer from fleeting lapses in their working memory when they are asked to perform even the most basic mental arithmetic. These same issues regarding memory were not present in the same students when they were required to answer questions that did not involve numbers. This very clearly demonstrated that the memory phenomenon is quite specific to only math.

So what exactly is it that causes this inhibiting math anxiety? Unfortunately it is not as simple as one answer, since math anxiety doesn't have one specific cause.

Frequently math anxiety can result of a student's either negative experience or embarrassment with math or a math teacher in previous years.

These circumstances can prompt the student to believe that he or she is somehow deficient in his or her math abilities. This belief will consistently lead to a poor performance in math tests and courses in general, leading only to confirm the beliefs of the student's inability. This particular phenomenon is referred to as the "self-fulfilling prophecy" by the psychological community. Math anxiety will result in poor performance, rather than it being the other way around.

Dr. Ashcraft stated that math anxiety is a "It's a learned, almost phobic, reaction to math," and that it is not only people prone to anxiety, fear, or panic who can develop math anxiety. The image alone of doing math problems can send the blood pressure and heart rate to race, even in the calmest person.

The study by Dr. Ashcraft and his colleague Elizabeth P. Kirk, discovered that students who suffered from math anxiety were frequently stumped by issues of even the most basic math rules, such as "carrying over" a number, when performing a sum, or "borrowing" from a number when doing a subtraction. Lapses such as this occurred only on working memory questions involving numbers.

To explain the problem with memory, Ashcraft states that when math anxiety begins to take its effect, the sufferer experiences a rush of thoughts, leaving little room for the focus required to perform even the simplest of math problems. He stated that "you're draining away the energy you need for solving the problem by worrying about it."

The outcome is a "vicious cycle," for students who are sufferers of math anxiety. As math anxiety is developed, the fear it promotes stands in the way of learning, leading to a decrease in self-confidence in the ability to perform even simple arithmetic.

A large portion of the problem lies in the ways in which math is taught to students today. In the US, students are frequently taught the rules of math, but rarely will they learn why a specific approach to a math problems work. Should students be provided with a foundation of "deeper understanding" of math, it may prevent the development of phobias.

Another study that was published in the Journal of Experimental Psychology by Dr. Jamie Campbell and Dr. Qilin Xue of the University of Saskatchewan in Saskatoon, Canada, reflected the same concepts. The researchers in this study looked at university students who were educated in Canada and China, discovering that the Chinese students could generally outperform the Canadian-educated students when it came to solving complex math problems involving procedural knowledge - the ability to know how to solve a math problem, instead of simply having ideas memorized.

A portion of this result seemed to be due to the use of calculators within both elementary and secondary schools; while Canadians frequently used them, the Chinese students did not.

However, calculators were not the only issue. Since Chinese-educated students also outperformed Canadian-educated students in complex math, it is suggested that cultural factors may also have an impact. However, the short-cut of using the calculator may hinder the development of the problem solving skills that are key to performing well in math.

Though it is critical that students develop such fine math skills, it is easier said than done. It would involve an overhaul of the training among all elementary and secondary educators, changing the education major in every college.

Math Myths

One problem that contributes to the progression of math anxiety, is the belief of many math myths. These erroneous math beliefs include the following:

Men are better in math than women - however, research has failed to demonstrate that there is any difference in math ability between the sexes. There is a single best way to solve a math problem - however, the majority of math problems can be solved in a number of different ways. By saying that there is only one way to solve a math problem, the thinking and creative skills of the student are held back.

Some people have a math mind, and others do not - in truth, the majority of people have much more potential for their math capabilities than they believe of themselves.

It is a bad thing to count by using your fingers - counting by using fingers has actually shown that an understanding of arithmetic has been established. People who are skilled in math can do problems quickly in their heads - in actuality, even math professors will review their example problems before they teach them in their classes.

The anxieties formed by these myths can frequently be perpetuated by a range of mind games that students seem to play with themselves. These math mind games include the following beliefs:

I don't perform math fast enough - actually everyone has a different rate at which he or she can learn. The speed of the solving of math problems is not important as long as the student can solve it.

I don't have the mind for math - this belief can inhibit a student's belief in him or herself, and will therefore interfere with the student's real ability to learn math.

I got the correct answer, but it was done the wrong way - there is no single best way to complete a math problem. By believing this, a student's creativity and overall understanding of math is hindered.

If I can get the correct answer, then it is too simple - students who suffer from math anxiety frequently belittle their own abilities when it comes to their math capabilities.

Math is unrelated to my "real" life - by freeing themselves of the fear of math, math anxiety sufferers are only limiting their choices and freedoms for the rest of their life.

Fortunately, there are many ways to help those who suffer from math anxiety. Since math anxiety is a learned, psychological response to doing or thinking about math, that interferes with the sufferer's ability to understand and perform math, it is not at all a reflection of the sufferer's true math sills and abilities.

Helpful Strategies

Many strategies and therapies have been developed to help students to overcome their math anxious responses. Some of these helpful strategies include the following:

Reviewing and learning basic arithmetic principles, techniques and methods. Frequently math anxiety is a result of the experience of many students with early negative situations, and these students have never truly developed a strong base in basic arithmetic, especially in the case of multiplication and fractions. Since math is a discipline that is built on an accumulative foundation, where the concepts are built upon gradually from simpler concepts, a student who has not achieved a solid basis in arithmetic will experience difficulty in learning higher order math. Taking a remedial math course, or a short math course that focuses on arithmetic can often make a considerable difference in reducing the anxious response that math anxiety sufferers have with math.

Becoming aware of any thoughts, actions and feelings that are related to math and responses to math. Math anxiety has a different effect on different students. Therefore it is very important to become familiar with any reactions that the math anxiety sufferer may have about him/herself and the situation when math has been encountered. If the sufferer becomes aware of any irrational or unrealistic thoughts, it's possible to better concentrate on replacing these thoughts with more positive and realistic ones.

Find help! Math anxiety, as we've mentioned, is a learned response, that is reinforced repeatedly over a period of time, and is therefore not something that can be eliminated instantaneously. Students can more effectively reduce their anxious responses with the help of many different services that are readily available. Seeking the assistance of a psychologist or counselor, especially one with a specialty in math anxiety, can assist the sufferer in performing an analysis of his/her psychological response to math, as well as learning anxiety management skills, and developing effective coping strategies. Other great tools are tutors, classes that teach better abilities to take better notes in math class, and other math learning aids.

Learning the mathematic vocabulary will instantly provide a better chance for understanding new concepts. One major issue among students is the lack of understanding of the terms and vocabulary that are common jargon within math classes. Typically math classes will utilize words in a completely different way from the way in which they are utilized in all other subjects. Students easily mistake their lack of understanding the math terms with their mathematical abilities.

Learning anxiety reducing techniques and methods for anxiety management. Anxiety greatly interferes with a student's ability to concentrate, think clearly, pay attention, and remember new concepts. When these same students can learn to relax, using anxiety management techniques, the student can regain his or her ability to control his or her emotional and physical symptoms of anxiety that interfere with the capabilities of mental processing.

Working on creating a positive overall attitude about mathematics. Looking at math with a positive attitude will reduce anxiety through the building of a positive attitude.

Learning to self-talk in a positive way. Pep talking oneself through a positive self talk can greatly assist in overcoming beliefs in math myths or the mind games that may be played. Positive self-talking is an effective way to replace the negative thoughts - the ones that create the anxiety. Even if the sufferer doesn't believe the statements at first, it plants a positive seed in the subconscious, and allows a positive outlook to grow.

Beyond this, students should learn effective math class, note taking and studying techniques. Typically, the math anxious students will avoid asking questions to save themselves from embarrassment. They will sit in the back of classrooms, and refrain from seeking assistance from the professor. Moreover, they will put off studying for math until the very last moment, since it causes them such substantial discomfort. Alone, or a combination of these negative behaviors work only to reduce the anxiety of the students, but in reality, they are actually building a substantially more intense anxiety.

There are many different positive behaviors that can be adopted by math anxious students, so that they can learn to better perform within their math classes.

Sit near the front of the class. This way, there will be fewer distractions, and there will be more of a sensation of being a part of the topic of discussion.
If any questions arise, ASK! If one student has a question, then there are certain to be others who have the same question but are too nervous to ask - perhaps because they have not yet learned how to deal with their own math anxiety.

Seek extra help from the professor after class or during office hours.

Prepare, prepare, prepare - read textbook material before the class, do the homework and work out any problems available within the textbook. Math skills are developed through practice and repetition, so the more practice and repetition, the better the math skills.

Review the material once again after class, to repeat it another time, and to reinforce the new concepts that were learned.

Beyond these tactics that can be taken by the students themselves, teachers and parents need to know that they can also have a large impact on the reduction of math anxiety within students.

As parents and teachers, there is a natural desire to help students to learn and understand how they will one day utilize different math techniques within their everyday lives. But when the student or teacher displays the symptoms of a person who has had nightmarish memories regarding math, where hesitations then develop in the instruction of students, these fears are automatically picked up by the students and commonly adopted as their own.

However, it is possible for teachers and parents to move beyond their own fears to better educate students by overcoming their own hesitations and learning to enjoy math.

Begin by adopting the outlook that math is a beautiful, imaginative or living thing. Of course, we normally think of mathematics as numbers that can be added or subtracted, multiplied or divided, but that is simply the beginning of it.

By thinking of math as something fun and imaginative, parents and teachers can teach children different ways to manipulate numbers, for example in balancing a checkbook. Parents rarely tell their children that math is everywhere around us; in nature, art, and even architecture. Usually, this is because they were never shown these relatively simple connections. But that pattern can break very simply through the participation of parents and teachers.

The beauty and hidden wonders of mathematics can easily be emphasized through a focus that can open the eyes of students to the incredible mathematical patterns that arise everywhere within the natural world. Observations and discussions can be made into things as fascinating as spider webs, leaf patterns, sunflowers and even coastlines. This makes math not only beautiful, but also inspiring and (dare we say) fun!

Pappas Method

For parents and teachers to assist their students in discovering the true wonders of mathematics, the techniques of Theoni Pappas can easily be applied, as per her popular and celebrated book "Fractals, Googols and Other Mathematical Tales." Pappas used to be a math phobia sufferer and created a fascinating step-by-step program for parents and teachers to use in order to teach students the joy of math.

Her simple, constructive step-by-step program goes as follows:

Don't let your fear of math come across to your kids - Parents must be careful not to perpetuate the mathematical myth - that math is only for specially talented "math types." Strive not to make comments like; "they don't like math" or "I have never been good at math." When children overhear comments like these from their primary role models they begin to dread math before even considering a chance of experiencing its wonders. It is important to encourage your children to read and explore the rich world of mathematics, and to practice mathematics without imparting negative biases.

Don't immediately associate math with computation (counting) - It is very important to realize that math is not just numbers and computations, but a realm of exciting ideas that touch every part of our lives -from making a telephone call to how the hair grows on someone's head. Take your children outside and point out real objects that display math concepts. For example, show them the symmetry of a leaf or angles on a building. Take a close look at the spirals in a spider web or intricate patterns of a snowflake.

Help your child understand why math is important - Math improves problem solving, increases competency and should be applied in different ways. It's the same as reading. You can learn the basics of reading without ever enjoying a novel. But, where's the excitement in that? With math, you could stop with the basics. But why when there is so much more to be gained by a fuller Understanding? Life is so much more enriching when we go beyond the basics. Stretch your children's minds to become involved in mathematics in ways that will not only be practical but also enhance their lives.

Make math as "hands on" as possible - Mathematicians participate in mathematics. To really experience math encourage your child to dig in and tackle problems in creative ways. Help them learn how to manipulate numbers using concrete references they understand as well as things they can see or touch. Look for patterns everywhere, explore shapes and symmetries. How many octagons do you see each day on the way to the grocery store? Play math puzzles and games and then encourage your child to try to invent their own. And, whenever possible, help your child realize a mathematical conclusion with real and tangible results. For example, measure out a full glass of juice with a measuring cup and then ask your child to drink half. Measure what is left. Does it measure half of a cup?

Read books that make math exciting:

Fractals, Googols and Other Mathematical Tales introduces an animated cat who explains fractals, tangrams and other mathematical concepts you've probably never heard of to children in terms they can understand. This book can double as a great text book by using one story per lesson.

A Wrinkle in Time is a well-loved classic, combining fantasy and science.

The Joy of Mathematics helps adults explore the beauty of mathematics that is all around.

The Math Curse is an amusing book for 4-8 year olds.

The Gnarly Gnews is a free, humorous bi-monthly newsletter on mathematics.

The Phantom Tollbooth is an Alice in Wonderland-style adventure into the worlds of words and numbers.

Use the internet to help your child explore the fascinating world of mathematics.
Web Math provides a powerful set of math-solvers that gives you instant answers to the stickiest problems.
Math League has challenging math materials and contests for fourth grade and above.
Silver Burdett Ginn Mathematics offers Internet-based math activities for grades K-6.
The Gallery of Interactive Geometry is full of fascinating, interactive geometry activities.

Math is very much like a language of its own. And like any second language, it will get rusty if it is not practiced enough. For that reason, students should always be looking into new ways to keep understanding and brushing up on their math skills, to be certain that foundations do not crumble, inhibiting the learning of new levels of math.

There are many different books, services and websites that have been developed to take the fear out of math, and to help even the most uncertain student develop self confidence in his or her math capabilities.

There is no reason for math or math classes to be a frightening experience, nor should it drive a student crazy, making them believe that they simply don't have the "math brain" that is needed to solve certain problems.

There are friendly ways to tackle such problems and it's all a matter of dispelling myths and creating a solid math foundation.

Concentrate on re-learning the basics and feeling better about yourself in math, and you'll find that the math brain you've always wanted, was there all along.

Special Report: Additional Bonus Material

Due to our efforts to try to keep this book to a manageable length, we've created a link that will give you access to all of your additional bonus material.

Please visit http://www.mometrix.com/bonus948/postal/ to access the information.

SCOTT CANDLER